THE
NEW EARTH
BOOK

THE
NEW EARTH
BOOK

OUR CHANGING PLANET

by MELVIN BERGER

Illustrated by George DeGrazio

Thomas Y. Crowell   New York

The New Earth Book: Our Changing Planet
Text copyright © 1980 by Melvin Berger
Illustrations copyright © 1980 by George DeGrazio
All rights reserved. Printed in the United States of America.
No part of this book may be used or reproduced in any manner
whatsoever without written permission except in the case of
brief quotations embodied in critical articles and reviews.
For information address Crowell Junior Books, 10 East 53rd Street,
New York, N. Y. 10022. Published simultaneously in Canada by
Fitzhenry & Whiteside Limited, Toronto.
Designed by Amelia Lau

Library of Congress Cataloging in Publication Data
Berger, Melvin.
The new earth book.
Bibliography: p.
Includes index.
SUMMARY: This introduction to the earth explores
such subjects as the shifting continents, mountain
building, earthquakes, the atmosphere, and pollution.
1. Earth sciences—Juvenile literature.
[1. Earth sciences] I. DeGrazio, George. II. Title.
OE29.B47   1980   550   79–7828
ISBN 0–690–00735–7
ISBN 0–690–04074–1 (lib. bdg.)

1   2   3   4   5   6   7   8   9   10

First Edition

For Ellie and Nancy, with love

CONTENTS

INTRODUCING
THE EARTH

OUR PUZZLING PLANET EARTH. It came into being about 5 billion years ago. It will last perhaps another 5 billion years.

Without the sun, a nearby star, it would be no more than a frozen ball of rock and metal in space. With the sun it is able to support many millions of different types of living plants and animals.

The earth is a round globe, but its surface looks flat to the people who live on it. Speeding through space at 65,000 miles per hour (105,000 km), it seems to be standing still.

Although it is called planet earth, some say that it should more properly be called planet water, since nearly three-quarters of its surface is covered with water.

The continents, which seem so permanent and unmoving, float on softer rock beneath the surface of the earth.

The temperature inside the earth is so high that solid rock can melt there, while the temperature at the South Pole often drops to 100° F below zero $(-73°\,C)$.

As long as there have been people on earth, they have tried to understand the planet on which they live. But earth did not give up its secrets easily.

In the early days, people created myths and legends to explain the world around them. Later, with the rise of science, some brilliant thinkers were able to find the first natural explanations of happenings on earth.

Recently there has been a dramatic advance in our knowledge of the earth. New tools and methods have vastly increased our insights. There have been major breakthroughs in our understanding of the creation and probable destruction of the earth, of its exact size, shape, and constitution, and of its movements through space.

We are learning that the earth is always changing. Earthquakes, volcanoes, and powerful forces deep within the earth are at work building mountains, creating oceans, moving continents, altering the shape and form of the earth. And we are finding out how life, in all its variety, has grown and developed to fit in with the ever-changing conditions on earth.

This book, then, is an exploration of what we know about our planet earth, with a special mention of what we have recently discovered.

THE EARTH
IN SPACE

ABOUT 5 BILLION YEARS ago, a giant cloud of dust and gas was floating about in space. It stretched billions and billions of miles from one end to the other.

Ever so slowly, over millions of years, the cloud began to shrink. It was made smaller by gravity. Gravity is the force that attracts all matter and all objects to one another. It pulled the vast cloud into an immense ball of superhot gas, with a diameter somewhat less than 1 million miles (1.6 million km).

When it reached this size and shape, it became a star. We

call this particular star the sun. The sun poured out great amounts of heat and light, as well as other kinds of energy.

Soon after the sun was formed, a number of smaller bodies began to travel around the sun. We call these bodies planets.

No one is sure how the planets were formed. Some scientists say that another large star passed close to the sun. The pull of gravity between this star and the sun was so powerful that it ripped out big clouds of gas from both of them. These clouds then formed the planets.

Other scientists believe that not all of the giant cloud of dust and gas was drawn into the sphere of the sun when the sun was forming. Some remained outside and later formed the planets. Just now this theory is the one that is the most popular among scientists.

Planet Earth

The earth is a large round ball or sphere. It is not, however, a perfect sphere. It is slightly flat at the North and South poles, and it bulges slightly at the equator, the imaginary line around the middle of the earth. Scientists call it an oblate sphere, meaning a slightly flattened sphere. They compare it to a beach ball that is not fully blown up.

Because the earth is an oblate sphere, it measures slightly less from pole to pole than between opposite points on the equator. The difference, though, is very small. The diameter of the earth from pole to pole is 7,900 miles (12,714 km). The distance between two opposite points on the equator is 7,926 miles (12,756 km).

In recent years, several new and more exact measurements of earth have been made by using man-made satellites. According to one recent measurement, the North Pole is about 80 feet (24.4 m) farther from the center of the earth than the South Pole. This means that the Northern Hemisphere is a tiny bit longer than the Southern Hemisphere. Our latest picture of the earth is of an oblate sphere with a hint of a pear shape.

The Earth and the Sun

The sun is the main source of energy for the earth. It pours out radiant energy in all directions. Although only a tiny fraction of the sun's enormous energy reaches the earth, it supplies most of our energy needs. Without light, none of the earth's green plants would be able to grow. Many animals would not be able to find food and would die. Without heat from the sun, the earth would be lifeless.

Besides the direct light and heat energy, the sun also supplies indirect energy in the form of oil, gas, and coal. These fossil fuels were formed from plants or animals that depended upon the sun for their energy needs.

Light and heat are only two of the many kinds of energy emitted by the sun. The sun also emits large amounts of

ultraviolet light. Ultraviolet light has a shorter wavelength than the waves of visible light. Ultraviolet light cannot be seen or felt. Yet it can be dangerous to living beings. If you spend too much time in the sun, you may get a severe sunburn caused by ultraviolet light.

X rays are even shorter than ultraviolet waves. X rays can also cause great damage to living tissue. These rays have so much energy that they are able to pass through matter. Doctors and dentists use this property of X rays to see inside the body. They have special X-ray machines that send X rays through bones or teeth, and onto photographic film. The results are X-ray pictures that show inner details that are otherwise hidden from view.

The shortest- and highest-energy waves from the sun are the gamma rays. They are the most penetrating and the most destructive to life.

In addition to all the waves and rays that come from the

Aurora borealis

sun, there are also tiny bits of matter, called particles. These particles come from within the atoms of the gases that make up the sun. They are mostly protons and electrons.

These particles from the sun form the solar wind. The solar wind goes out in all directions, including toward the earth. The layer of air around the earth and the earth's natural magnetism protect us from most of the solar wind. Delicate measuring instruments in space satellites above the earth's atmosphere have only recently succeeded in detecting the solar wind.

As the solar wind strikes the atoms in the air between 50 and 100 miles (80 and 160 km) above the North and South poles, it causes them to give off light. These glowing lights in the extreme northern and southern skies are called auroras (aurora borealis in the north, aurora australis in the south).

The solar wind is what makes the tails of comets always face away from the sun.

For some 5 billion years, the sun has been showering waves of energy and particles on earth. But the sun, like other stars, will change. It will grow much bigger. One day it will probably swallow up the planets Mercury and Venus. Then, with the sun so close to the earth, everything here will be burned to a cinder.

There is, however, no immediate danger. Scientists guess that it will be another 5 billion years before this happens.

The Earth and the Solar System

The earth is one of nine planets that circle the sun. All together the sun and planets make up the solar system. The

nine planets, starting closest to the sun, are Mercury, Venus, Earth, Mars, Jupiter, Saturn, Uranus, Neptune, and Pluto.

The sizes and distances within the solar system are immense. The sun has a diameter of 864,000 miles (1.4 million km). The distance between the earth and the sun is nearly 93 million miles (150 million km). If the sun were the size of a basketball, then the earth would be the size of a green pea.

The planets of the solar system are always moving at great speeds. They revolve in giant orbits around the sun. The earth, for example, revolves around the sun at just over 65,000 miles (105,000 km) per hour. The distance, though, is so great that it still takes the earth 365.25 days to make one complete revolution around the sun. This period of time, 365.25 days, we call a year.

The planets also spin, or rotate, as they revolve around the sun. The earth rotates around an imaginary axis that goes through the earth from the North Pole to the South Pole. It takes the earth twenty-four hours, or one day, to make one complete rotation.

As the earth rotates, roughly half of it gets the full light of the sun for about twelve hours. It is daytime for that half of the globe. The other half of the earth faces away from the sun for twelve hours. There it is dark, or nighttime.

The part of the earth facing the sun is warmed by the heat from the sun. At night, as it turns away from the sun, it cools off. That is why it is usually cooler at night than during the day.

Place a lamp without a shade near the center of a darkened room. The lamp represents the sun pouring out its radiation. Now hold a globe or a large ball in your hands to represent the earth.

Walk counterclockwise around the lamp. Support the ball at the top and bottom and spin it as you walk. Do you see how different parts of the spinning globe are lit and warmed by the lamp? On the earth, it is always day at the light parts, and night at the dark parts. If you could spin the globe 365 times as you walk once around the lamp, you would be representing the 365 days that make up a year on earth.

The earth's seasons change because the earth's axis is tilted at an angle of 23.5°. During part of the earth's journey around the sun, the northern half of the globe is tilted toward the sun. That part receives more radiant energy from

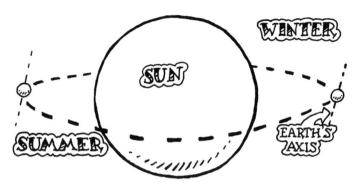

Seasons of the Northern Hemisphere

the sun because the sun's rays are more direct. It is warmer and the days are longer. It is spring and summer, which together last from about March 21 to September 21.

For the other half of the year, from September 21 to March 21, the northern half of the earth is tilted away from the sun. The sun's rays are less direct and the daylight hours are shorter. The weather is cooler. It is fall and winter in the northern half of the world.

You can use the lamp and ball to try this out. Mark a point on the ball to represent the North Pole and hold the ball so that the North Pole is slightly tilted toward the lamp. Do you see how much brighter the light shines on the top of the ball than on the lower part? In the same way, the northern half of the earth, or the Northern Hemisphere, gets more of the sun's energy when the North Pole is tilted toward the sun.

Now slowly rotate the ball the way the earth rotates but keep the same tilt. Do you see how the top part spends more time in the light than the bottom part? That shows why days are longer during the spring and summer in the Northern Hemisphere, when the North Pole is tilted toward the sun.

When the Northern Hemisphere is tilted toward the sun, the Southern Hemisphere is tilted away from the sun. The sun strikes the Southern Hemisphere at an angle. The less direct rays give less heat. The days are shorter, not allowing the land to be warmed. Thus, while it is spring and summer in the Northern Hemisphere, it is fall and winter in the Southern Hemisphere. For the other half of the year, the seasons are reversed. While it is spring and summer in the Southern Hemisphere, it is fall and winter in the north.

On June 21, the Northern Hemisphere is tilted toward the sun the most. Yet that part of the earth reaches its highest temperatures in July and August. Why? The reason is that it takes until July and August for the sun's heat to warm up the earth. In the winter, on December 21, the Northern Hemisphere is tilted away from the sun the most. The coldest weather, though, comes in January and February, when the Northern Hemisphere has lost the most heat.

The Earth and the Moon

The body closest to earth in space is the moon, about 239,000 miles (384,000 km) away. It takes about twenty-nine days for the moon to make one complete revolution around the earth. A month (from the word "moon") is the time of one revolution.

The moon also makes one rotation on its axis in the time it takes to make one revolution around the earth. That is why the same side of the moon is turned toward earth at all times.

The moon is a sphere with a diameter of 2,160 miles (3,476 km), about one-fourth that of earth. Yet the sun, which is about 400 times as large as the moon, appears the same size in the sky. It looks the same because the sun is about 400 times farther away from earth than the moon is.

Here is a simple experiment that will show you why the sun and the moon look the same size. You will need two sheets of notebook paper, a yardstick, and a friend to help you. With tape or a thumbtack, attach one sheet of paper to a wall. Fold the other piece of paper in half. Stand about a yard from the wall, holding the folded piece of paper in front of you. Block out part of the sheet on the wall. Move it back and forth until it appears to be the same length as the paper on the wall.

Now ask your friend to measure the distances from your eye to the folded paper, and from the folded paper to the paper on the wall. It is twice as far from the paper to the wall as it is from your eye to the folded paper. This is because the paper on the wall is twice as long. The moon and sun appear to be the same size even though the sun is 400 times bigger because the sun is 400 times farther away.

Like the earth, the moon gets its light from the sun. The sun always lights up the same part of the moon. As the moon circles the earth, you can see more and more of the sunlit

Phases of the moon

Eclipse of the moon

part. The varying amounts of lit-up surface, as seen from the earth, are known as the phases of the moon.

As the earth revolves around the sun, it casts its shadow off into space. When the earth moves between the sun and the moon, its shadow falls on the moon. An eclipse of the moon takes place. Such eclipses occur between two and five times a year.

An eclipse of the sun occurs when the moon comes between the sun and the earth. A total eclipse of the sun takes place when the moon completely covers the face of the sun. This occurs somewhere on earth every one to five years. Partial eclipses of the sun are much more common.

Both the sun and the moon appear to rise in the east and set in the west because the earth rotates on its axis from west

Eclipse of the sun

to east. Because of the relationship between the earth's rotation and the moon's orbit, the moon appears to rise about fifty minutes later each day.

The moon's gravity, and to a lesser extent that of the sun, exerts a "pull" on the earth. This pull causes tides, the rise and fall of ocean waters.

High tides occur on the side of the earth that faces the moon. As the earth rotates on its axis, the "tidal bulge" moves around the globe. High tides come to most places on earth about twice a day.

From its lowest point, the water rises slowly for about six hours until it reaches high tide. Then, for the next six hours, it falls gradually, until it reaches low tide. The cycle repeats itself over and over again.

High tides are higher than usual when the pull of the sun's gravity is added to the pull of the moon's gravity. This occurs when both bodies are pulling along the same line, as they do at full moon and new moon. When the tide rises higher than normal, it is called a spring tide. (Spring tide has nothing to do with the spring season.) Twice a month the pull of the sun and the pull of the moon are at right angles to each other. Then the tides are lower than normal. These are called neap tides.

Tides also occur on the side of the earth facing away from the moon. In part, the water bulges out because the moon pulls the land slightly away from the water.

The gravity that causes tides affects all bodies of water, large and small. The changing level of the water, though, is noticed mostly along the ocean coasts. Here the movement of the tides helps clean beaches and harbors. It picks up waste from the edges of the ocean and carries it to deep water, where it slowly sinks to the bottom.

The tides are slowing down the rotational speed of the earth a tiny fraction of a second every year. This slowdown is caused by the friction of the moving water in the tidal bulge against the ocean floors. At the present rate of slowdown, a day will be twenty-four hours and one second long by the year 7000!

Scientists recently found winds, called lunar winds, above the surface of the earth. These winds are too weak to be felt, but they have been detected with delicate instruments. In places where measurements have been made, scientists have found that the air pressure rises and falls twice a day, just as the ocean tides do. The difference in air pressure, though, is very small—only about 0.001 inch (0.025 mm) of mercury.

The Earth in the Universe

The planets and sun of our solar system are only a tiny speck in the vast reaches of the Milky Way galaxy. A galaxy is an immense group of stars that move through space together. There are about 100 billion stars in the Milky Way galaxy. Our sun is a very ordinary, average star among this vast number of stars.

The Milky Way galaxy is one of perhaps 600 billion galaxies. These galaxies stretch out over trillions and trillions of miles in space. All together, these galaxies, and everything that is in them, make up the universe.

Scientists believe that the universe is much older than the earth and the solar system. According to their latest findings, the universe is between 10 and 15 billion years old. Before then, all the matter in the universe was packed into a gigantic ball. Then there was a tremendous explosion, called the Big Bang, which sent all the matter flying out into space. All the galaxies, stars, and planets have been and are being formed from this matter as it rushes out through space.

As scientists have studied the theory of the Big Bang, they have come up with another theory. They say that, in time, the matter will stop flying out from the Big Bang. It will be pulled in by the force of gravity and begin to come closer together again. After about 80 billion years, they guess, all matter will be back in a ball like the one that originally exploded with the Big Bang. The earth will, of course, disappear, assuming that it survives that long.

In studying the vast reaches of the universe, scientists are quite sure that there are a number of stars similar to the sun and planets similar to earth. Among all the planets in the universe, there are surely some that are able to support some sort of life. Scientists are now trying to pick up any radio signals that may have been beamed to earth by living creatures on another planet. At the same time, they are sending out radio signals from earth to outer space in the hope that they will be received on some distant planet.

Compared to the immense universe, the earth is a very small speck. But to us, planet earth is home, and the most important place of all.

THE EARTH'S CRUST

THE CRUST IS THE EARTH'S outer surface. It is made up of solid rock, known as bedrock. The crust makes up most of what is called the lithosphere, or sphere of rock.

The lithosphere is formed from minerals, which are non-living chemical materials. Oxygen and silicon are the most abundant elements in most minerals.

In some places on land, usually on the side of a mountain, you can actually see the bedrock. Such exposed bedrock is called either an outcrop or an exposure. Most of the rocks you see, though, even the very largest boulders, are broken off from the bedrock.

The surface of the earth has a total area of nearly 200

million square miles (517 million sq. km). Only about 57 million square miles (148 million sq. km) are solid land. These are the continents. Here the crust is between 20 and 40 miles (33 and 66 km) thick. It is covered with a layer of soil, sand, broken rocks, or mud.

Most of the earth's surface, over 70 percent, is covered with water that forms oceans, lakes, and rivers. The crust under the oceans is only between 3 and 20 miles (5 and 33 km) thick.

Weathering

The earth's rocky crust is always under attack. Water, changes in temperature, wind, plants, animals, and chemicals break up the rock in a process known as weathering. It is a process that goes on all the time.

Weathering occurs when water seeps into a crack in a rock and then freezes. As water freezes, it expands. The force of the expanding water may be strong enough to split apart solid rock.

To see the force of freezing water for yourself, completely fill a small screw-on-top bottle with water. Place the bottle in a heavy brown-paper supermarket bag and wrap the bag around the bottle many times. Then put the wrapped bottle into the freezer part of your refrigerator overnight.

The next day, take out the bag and carefully remove the bottle. Is the water frozen into a solid block of ice? Did the expanding force of the water shatter the glass as it froze?

Just as water that freezes can split rocks, so plants can grow through cracks in rocks and break them apart. You have probably seen weeds pushing through paved roads or sidewalks. A walk through the woods will probably uncover a few examples of trees growing out of boulders. The slow growth of plants or trees is often strong enough to tear apart the hardest rock.

This experiment will show you the force of a growing plant. You will need a few pea or bean seeds, a cupful of plaster of paris, an empty tin can, and water. Soak the seeds overnight so they will be ready to sprout. The next day, mix the plaster of paris with water in the can to make it like thick mud. Place the seeds about one-quarter inch beneath the surface of the plaster. Leave the can in a warm place.

Within hours the plaster will harden and become solid.

In a few days the seeds will sprout. Then, as the tiny plants force their way up through the plaster, cracks will appear on the surface. The plants force their way through the plaster as other plants do through rocks.

Changes in air temperature also contribute to weathering. Most rocks contain two or more different minerals. Each mineral expands and contracts at slightly different rates with changes in temperature. This movement within the rocks can rip them apart. It usually causes the rock surface to crack and flake off in layers in a process called exfoliation.

By itself, the wind does little harm to rocks. But when the wind blows grains of sand, it works like sandpaper on wood, grinding away the surfaces of the rocks.

People break up rocks by digging or blasting, or by releasing chemical pollutants into the air. Burrowing animals loosen or remove the soil that surrounds or supports a rock. This allows the rock to be broken more easily by some other means. Some rocks crumble when plants growing over them produce acids that dissolve rock.

Various chemicals found naturally in the air and water can also dissolve and eat away at rocks. Rain and flowing rivers can cause them to fall apart.

The weathering of rocks over many, many years creates soil, the brownish, reddish layer that covers most of the earth's land area. Soil is a very complex material that varies from place to place. It is largely mineral, but its exact type depends on the kind of bedrock it comes from.

Most soils also contain large numbers of living things. There are the tiny bacteria that bring about the decay of dead plants and animals. This decayed material, called humus, enriches the soil and makes it better for growing plants. There are also many worms, ants, and beetles that tunnel through the soil. They break up the soil, allowing air and water to pass through.

Air and water in the soil are necessary for plant growth. If soil is too tightly packed, neither of these important materials is able to enter the soil. If the soil is too loosely packed, the water drips right through and is not available for plants.

Erosion

The process of carrying weathered material from one place to another is called erosion. The weathered material ranges from soil to sand, from giant boulders to tiny pebbles. It is usually moved along by flowing water, moving ice, or blowing wind.

Running water is the most important and widespread agent of erosion. All water, of course, flows downhill, from higher ground to lower ground.

When a new stream of water starts to flow, it first cuts into the soil and forms tiny little valleys, called gullies. From these gullies a single main stream usually develops with a narrow, deep valley. The stream is straight, often with a number of waterfalls and rapids.

Over hundreds or thousands of years, the stream, which is now called a river, widens and deepens. Eventually it creates a flat valley bottom, called a flood plain. The river now begins to follow a crooked path over the flood plain. Sometimes the river will make some U-turns that are later cut off from the rest of the river. They form separate lakes, called oxbow lakes. By now, the river has entered its old age.

All during its life a river erodes the land. Rivers carry loose soil, sand, gravel, and boulders, and deposit these materials in new places. Such deposits are called sediment. The sediment can form giant deltas, such as the one at the mouth of the Mississippi River.

In cold climates, the snow may pile up year after year and gradually change to ice because of the pressure and partial melting on the lower layers. The ice, which is a solid, begins to flow as though it were a thick, heavy liquid. The movement is so slow that it cannot be seen. A mass of slowly flowing ice is called a glacier.

Glaciers push and drag great quantities of rock as they move, sometimes smoothing the surface of the land, sometimes gouging out deep scratches, grooves, and valleys.

Some glaciers flow to the sea. When they reach the sea, great blocks of ice break off. These giant masses, called icebergs, float in the ocean until they melt.

Right now, glaciers cover about 10 percent of the earth's surface. In the past, though, during the ice ages, glaciers covered even more of the earth. Up until about 11,000 years ago, most of Canada and the northern United States was covered by glaciers. Scientists think these glaciers were formed about one million years before that.

Icebergs

Wind erosion is most damaging in dry desert areas where there is little plant life to hold the soil. The wind picks up the sand and dust particles and carries them, sometimes for hundreds of miles. Particles that are too heavy to be carried by the wind may be rolled or bounced along the ground.

Erosion, then, moves rock that has been broken down into smaller pieces by weathering. But how is rock formed in the first place?

Igneous Rocks

Beneath the earth's surface crust is a hot, thick, heavy liquid called magma. Magma is melted rock. The rock is melted by the great heat below the surface. When magma cools, it hardens and becomes solid rock. Rocks formed in this way are called igneous. Igneous means "produced by fire."

Magma cools off and becomes solid rock in two different

ways. Some remains beneath the surface and slowly loses its heat. It becomes intrusive or plutonic rock. The minerals in intrusive rocks form into large crystals. These rocks are usually rough and coarse-grained.

Some magma cools off after it rises to the surface. This rock, called lava or extrusive rock, cools quickly in the air. This allows less time for large crystals to form.

You can see how the two types of igneous rocks form in an experiment. Although the experiment is a simple one, it should be done with the help of an adult. You will need two test tubes, four mothballs, and a colored crayon. Put two mothballs and half the crayon, without the paper wrapping, into each test tube. These are the materials from which your rocks will be made.

Set the two test tubes (or two aluminum muffin tins, if no test tubes are available) in a beaker (or pan) of water. Heat the water to boiling in order to melt the materials in the test tubes. This is like the earth's heat melting the minerals beneath the surface.

When the materials have melted, turn off the heat. Leave one test tube in the hot water. That is like the magma cooling slowly beneath the surface. Remove the other test tube and place it in a beaker of cold water. That is like the magma coming to the surface and cooling quickly in the air.

When both test tubes have cooled, compare the smoothness of the two samples and the size of the crystals. Which is rough and coarse with bigger crystals, like intrusive rock? Which is smooth and less crystalline, like extrusive rock?

Sedimentary Rocks

Most scientists agree that originally all of the rock of the earth's crust was igneous rock. But they estimate that now about 75 percent of the rock is a different kind, called sedimentary rock.

Sedimentary rock begins to form when weathering breaks apart rocks that are on the surface of the earth. Then, by erosion, particularly by the action of rivers, these weathered pieces of rock are deposited as layers of sediment on the bottom of bodies of water. Natural cements dissolved in the water and the weight of the material above the sediment join the separate bits of rock and sand together into solid slabs of rock.

You can try an experiment that will show you how sedimentary rocks form. You will need three paper cups, some sand or small pebbles, some white liquid glue, and water.

Punch a number of small holes in one paper cup and fill it with the sand. In another cup mix two parts glue and one part water. This represents the natural cement dissolved in the water.

Now pour the glue–water mixture over the sand. Some will stick; most will run out through the holes. Catch the runoff in the third cup. Wait a few minutes and then pour the glue–water mixture over the sand again. Repeat several times, until most of the glue and water is used up. Set the cup of sand aside overnight and throw away the other two cups.

The next day, tear away the paper cup. Do you see how the sand has been formed into a rock? It is not smooth like igneous rocks. It is a sedimentary rock, formed by the glue dissolved in the water passing over the separate grains of sand.

Some sedimentary rocks are formed by chemical action. As water passes over some rocks it dissolves some of the minerals they contain. The minerals seem to disappear into the water. But later, when the water evaporates, the minerals that had been dissolved appear and are formed into new rocks.

Here is a simple experiment that illustrates the chemical formation of sedimentary rock. Dissolve a teaspoon of regular table salt in one-half cup of warm water. The salt disappears in the water. Put the cup in a warm place so that the water will quickly evaporate. After all the water has evaporated, look for solid grains of salt at the bottom of the cup.

The salt dissolved in water just as minerals in rocks dissolve in water. The salt later appeared as solid grains again, just as solid minerals appear again when the water in which they are dissolved is evaporated.

Sedimentary rocks are also formed from the remains of plants and animals that once lived on earth. The best known of these organic sedimentary rocks, as they are called, is coal.

Coal is formed from the plants—ferns, mosses, and trees —that grew in swamp waters millions of years ago. As these plants died, they were buried in thick layers. Over the years, the process of decay and the weight of the layers of sand and

soil that piled up on top turned the dead plant material into the organic sedimentary rock known as coal.

Organic limestone is formed from the shells of sea creatures that lived in the waters along the ocean coasts. Included are clams, oysters, sea snails, and mussels. When they died, their shells fell to the bottom. Over the years, these shells were cemented together to form this type of limestone.

Sedimentary rocks form very slowly. Quite often, the remains of dead animals and plants fall into the sediment as it is being formed. The rock then hardens with an impression of the animals or plants permanently set in or on the rock. These impressions in sedimentary rock are called fossils.

Scientists can tell a great deal about conditions on earth a long time ago by studying fossils. Fossils enable scientists to identify the different kinds of creatures that lived on earth, to trace changes in the types and numbers of living things, to map their distribution around the world, to learn about climate and other living conditions in the past, and much, much more.

Metamorphic Rocks

Sometimes sedimentary rocks are buried under great piles of sediment. Other times, earthquakes, volcanoes, or other upheavals on the earth's surface bury them. Eventually these sedimentary rocks become part of the crust of the earth. Heat and pressure change these rocks. They are then called metamorphic rocks ("meta" means change; "morphic" means shape or form).

Metamorphic rocks are usually harder and heavier than sedimentary rocks. Some of the more familiar metamorphic rocks are slate (which starts as shale, a sedimentary rock) and marble (originally limestone, also a sedimentary rock).

The Rock Cycle

The three types of rock—igneous, sedimentary, and metamorphic—are always changing, even though the changes may take place over thousands or millions of years. A typical cycle of change starts with igneous rock. Weathering and erosion create sediment from this rock. Natural forces change the sediment into sedimentary rock. Some of the sedimentary rock is forced beneath the surface of the earth, where it is changed into metamorphic rock.

During mountain building, movements of large masses of the earth's crust lead to some rock becoming buried deep beneath the surface. There great heat and pressure melt the rock, and it becomes magma.

Some of the magma cools and hardens. It becomes igneous rock. And the rock cycle starts again.

The next time you handle a piece of rock, think of its history: the elements of which the rock is made were created many billions of years ago. Since then, these elements may have passed through the rock cycle many times. The same rock may have been on the shore when the first sea creatures crawled out of the sea and onto the land. Dinosaurs may have trampled this rock. Perhaps at one time it exploded out of the earth in an erupting volcano. This rock that changed so much in the past may continue to change far into the future.

Land Pollution

Because of new rocks being formed and old rocks being destroyed by weathering, the crust of the earth is always changing. But over the last few centuries, as humans have cleared land for farms, built cities and roads, dug mines and dumped their wastes, they, too, have begun to change the earth's crust.

Before the twentieth century, the earth was able to overcome the effects of man's destructive activities. Most plants and animals were able to adjust both to the natural and to the man-made changes on the face of the earth. But some years ago, it became clear that the earth's living beings were not able to adjust to the rapidly changing—and worsening —conditions. The poisons and chemicals that people poured onto the earth's surface were killing living beings in the soil and making the soil useless for growing crops. Vast open garbage dumps were encouraging the growth of all sorts of germs, rodents, and insects. In many places, litter was piling up faster than it was being disposed of. Poorly planned cities and roads were destroying living places for animals and plants.

This spoiling of the earth is called land pollution. Pollution can lead to sickness and death for humans, animals, and plants. It can lead to the disappearance of some types of living beings. Also, as more land is polluted, there is less land for growing the plants that humans and animals need for food.

Around 1970, people realized that humans were polluting the land faster than nature could clean it up. Some individuals, industries, and governments began taking steps to clean up the mess and to prevent its spread. Antipollution actions, community planning, and the passage of certain laws have already stopped pollution from growing worse. Perhaps, with everyone's help, it will be possible to solve the earth's pollution problems.

INSIDE
THE EARTH

ONE WAY TO LEARN what is inside the earth is to dig a hole. But, because of the great size of the earth, you would have to dig down nearly 4,000 miles (6,500 km) just to reach the center of the earth. And you would need to dig twice as far to reach the other side.

The fact is that the deepest hole ever dug into the earth reaches down only 10 miles (16 km). Yet scientists know as much about the inside of the earth as if they had dug down farther. Almost everything they know about the earth's interior has been discovered by indirect means.

Layers of the Earth

The earth's crust is a thin layer. It ranges from 5 to 40 miles (8 to 64 km) in thickness.

Most of what goes on beneath the earth's surface has been discovered by the modern study of earthquake waves. Earthquakes are caused by sudden breaks or shifts of rocks on or near the surface of the earth. These changes produce waves of energy that spread out in all directions. The waves are picked up by scientific instruments at many different points on the surface of the earth.

The speed and direction of the waves is determined by the type of rock through which they pass. Careful measurements of earthquake waves have helped scientists to prepare a diagram of the inside of the earth.

This simple activity will show you how different conditions affect the speed and direction of a wave. Roll a round pencil down a slanted board. Notice how the pencil rolls straight down rather quickly.

Now cover part of the board with a towel and roll the pencil down again. Notice how the pencil moves more slowly and rolls off course as it passes over the towel.

In the same way, earthquake waves change their pattern as they pass through different materials inside the earth. By comparing the speed and direction of the waves as they are picked up at labs around the world, scientists can tell what types of materials the waves passed through.

In 1909, the Yugoslav scientist Andrija Mohorovičic discovered a change in the speed of earthquake waves a few miles beneath the earth's surface. It indicated a change in the type of rocks at that level. He estimated the level to be about 6 miles (10 km) below the seafloor, 12 miles (20 km) below the surface of the continents. This zone of change is now called the Moho, in honor of Mohorovičic.

Earthquake waves move faster beneath the Moho than in the crust. That is probably because the material under the Moho is heavier than the rock of the crust. This layer, called the mantle, occupies more than 80 percent of the total volume of the earth. It is about 1,800 miles (2,896 km) thick.

From laboratory research on rocks at the temperature and pressure thought to be in the mantle, scientists believe that the mantle is made up of heavy rock containing a great deal of the metals magnesium and iron. The heat and pressure in the mantle probably soften the rock, so that although it is solid, it can change shape.

A sudden change in the speed of earthquake waves shows another layer, the outer core, inside the mantle. The outer core extends from the mantle toward the center of the earth for about 1,350 miles (2,172 km). The faster movement of waves in this layer indicates that it is made of heavier material than the mantle. The outer core is probably made up mostly of the metals iron and nickel in a melted or liquid state.

The inner core, the next layer, reaches to the very center of the earth. It is about 800 miles (1,287 km) thick. Like the

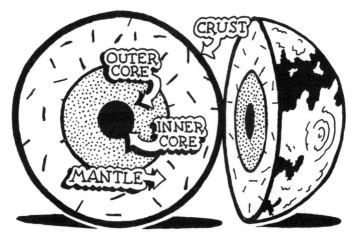

outer core, it is also composed of iron and nickel. But surprisingly enough, in the inner core, the two metals appear to be in a solid state.

Geothermal Energy

The temperature of the top 50 feet (15 m) of the earth's crust always stays the same. It is the same as the year-round average surface temperature for that area.

In some areas around the world, though, the rocks just under the surface are at much higher temperatures. Scientists believe that the rocks in these places contain large amounts of thorium and uranium, which are radioactive elements. The gradual decay of these elements releases heat. The heat is trapped in the rocks, and over millions of years it has built up to the present high levels.

The heat from the rocks may be used as a source of energy called geothermal energy. Geothermal energy usually takes one of three forms. The most valuable form occurs when water is trapped in heated rocks, where it is turned into steam. The steam forces its way to the surface, where it is used to turn the generators of a power plant in order to produce electricity.

Geothermal steam is very rare. Much more common are giant underground pools of water that are heated by the rocks but not turned into steam. This water is of less value than steam. Deep wells must be dug to get the water out, while the steam usually comes to the surface naturally. The heated water contains many dissolved minerals, which clog the pipes through which the water passes. And since it is not as hot as steam, it is not as efficient in running a generator, or even in heating buildings.

The most promising source of geothermal energy is the hot rock that is close to the surface in some areas. Here, engineers drill twin holes down to the hot rock. Through one hole they pump down clean water. The water is heated by the hot rock and comes up to the surface through the other hole, either as superheated water or as steam.

Heat and Pressure

The temperature below the earth's surface increases the farther down you go. Most scientists estimate that the temperature rises about 85° F (30° C) for every mile (1.6 km) of depth.

Over a short time, very little of the great heat within the earth reaches the surface. On a sunny day about 2,500 times as much energy comes from the sun.

In very rough figures, the temperature at the Moho level is around 2500° F (1400° C). The mantle averages 5000° F (2760° C). And the outer and the inner cores range from about 5400° F (3000° C) to perhaps 10,000° F (5500° C) at the earth's center.

Where does the great heat inside the earth come from? Why is it greater toward the center of the earth?

Some of the heat inside the earth originated when the earth was first formed. Since rocks lose their heat very slowly, they still retain some of their original heat—even after 5 billion years.

Most of the high temperatures are produced by the natural radioactivity of certain rocks in the earth's interior. These rocks contain elements, such as thorium and uranium, which are always emitting particles and rays, and producing heat. Although the percentage of radioactive elements is small, over the history of the earth they have produced a great deal of heat.

Scientists estimate that the pressure at the center of the earth is about 53 million pounds (24 million kg) per square inch (6.5 sq. cm). This great pressure, it is believed, prevents the iron of the inner core from melting, despite the high temperature.

In March 1978, scientists succeeded in creating a pressure of 25.2 million pounds (11.5 million kg) per square inch (6.5 sq. cm) in the laboratory. This tremendous pressure approaches the pressure found near the center of the earth. Under this pressure, a diamond, one of the hardest substances known, flowed like thick clay.

Further experiments with various substances under extraordinary pressure should give even more information about conditions at various layers under the surface of the earth. One of the first findings, announced in May 1980, was that the earth's core may not be formed of iron and nickel, but of iron and a lighter element, such as oxygen or sulfur.

Magnetism

The ancient Greeks discovered that certain rocks could attract metal. These rocks were really a type of iron ore. They called them magnets after Magnesia, the city in which they were first found.

About 1,000 years ago, the Chinese found that a magnet, placed where it could turn freely, would always line up in approximately a north–south line. This led to the invention of the compass, a most important help to sailors and travelers.

You can make your own compass. Take a bar magnet and tie a string around its middle so that it will remain horizontal when hung freely. Hold the magnet by the end of the string.

Notice that it always lines up in the same direction, no matter how much you twist or shake the string. Is your magnet marked to show which end points to the north? If not, can you figure out which direction is north and mark the end of the magnet that points in that direction?

Next cut a large circle out of a piece of paper. Fold it into quarters. Mark north, east, south, and west in a clockwise direction where each fold meets the edge. Place the paper under the magnet so that north on the paper is directly under the N pole of the magnet. Use your compass to locate points to the south, east, and west.

The earth is like one giant magnet, and the two magnetic poles are like the ends of this magnet. If you were to hold a bar magnet directly over the North Magnetic Pole, it would point straight down.

The compass points to the North and South Magnetic poles. They are about 825 miles (1,327 km) from the North and South Geographic poles, where all the lines of longitude come together.

The magnetism of the earth seems to come from the inner and outer cores. The outer core, you recall, is liquid iron and nickel. It is believed that these metals move slowly around the solid-metal inner core. As they move, they set up their own electrical currents. The electrical currents in the outer core turn the solid metal inner core into a magnet. It is like an iron bar that becomes magnetized when it is wrapped with wires carrying electrical current.

You can magnetize iron in this experiment. You will need a large iron nail, a length of insulated copper wire, and a dry cell battery.

Wind the copper wire around the iron nail at least twenty times. Scrape the insulation off the two ends of the wire and attach them to the terminals of the dry cell. Next, hold some paper clips near the nail. The current in the wire surrounding the nail has made the nail into a magnet. It is like the earth's inner core being made into a magnet by the electricity of the outer core.

Recent measurements show that the earth's magnetic poles do not always stay in the same place. They wander slightly over very long periods of time. Scientists think that shifts and movements of the earth's core cause the magnetic poles to change position.

The earth's magnetism does not only create two magnetic poles. It also creates a magnetic field, a region around a magnet where the magnetic force extends.

Here is how you can see a magnetic field. Place a magnet on a table and cover it with a large piece of cardboard.

Sprinkle iron filings over the cardboard. Do you see the filings take on a pattern? Tap the sides of the cardboard lightly. Do you see the filings form lines around the shape of the magnet? The lines are called the lines of force. They show the magnetic field of the magnet. They curve around the magnet from pole to pole just as the earth's magnetic field curves around the earth from magnetic pole to magnetic pole.

Scientists are able to observe tiny changes in the earth's magnetic field from day to day, even from hour to hour. They believe that these changes are caused by the solar wind, the stream of electrons and protons emitted by the sun.

During 1958, early in the program of sending artificial satellites into space, scientists discovered a huge doughnut-shaped zone of protons and electrons surrounding the earth. The shape of this zone followed closely the lines of force of the earth's magnetic field. Since this zone was discovered by Dr. James A. Van Allen of the State University of Iowa, it is called the Van Allen belt.

Now there are thought to be two belts of particles, an inner and an outer one. The first zone extends from about 600 to 5,000 miles (1,000 to 8,000 km) above the surface of the earth. The outer zone reaches from about 11,000 to 16,000 miles (17,800 to 25,700 km) above the earth. The sources of these particles are still not known for sure. The probable sources are giant eruptions on the surface of the sun, called solar flares; high-energy particles from outer space, called cosmic rays; and solar winds.

Gravity

Sir Isaac Newton first discovered the force of gravity. His law of gravitation states that there is an attraction between every bit of matter in the universe and every other bit of matter. Your weight, for example, is the measure of the attraction between the planet earth and your body.

Two factors affect the force of gravity. One is the mass of the two things being attracted to each other. The more mass in the two objects, the greater the pull of gravity. For example, a baby has less mass, or matter, in its body than you have. Therefore, there is less of a pull of gravity between it and the earth. Since weight is a measure of the pull of gravity, a baby weighs less than you. If you become an astronaut and go to the moon, you will find that you weigh less there. The moon has less mass than the earth, and therefore there is less gravitational attraction.

The other factor that affects gravity is distance. The shorter the distance between two objects, the greater the force of gravity. The sun has far greater mass than the earth, and its gravitation attraction is much stronger than that of earth. But the sun is so far away that we are held firmly on earth, instead of being pulled out in space to the sun.

Since the earth's gravity can be thought of as coming from the very center of the earth, the higher up you are, the weaker the gravity. Scientists use a very sensitive instrument, a gravimeter, to measure gravity on the earth. They have found, for example, that gravity is greater at the poles than at the equator because the poles are closer to the center of the earth. Likewise, gravity is stronger at sea level than on top of a mountain.

But there are also places where two points, at exactly the same height, show a difference in gravity. This difference is caused by the makeup of the underlying rocks. The pull of gravity is greater over heavy, dense rocks than over light rocks. In some cases, a low gravity reading indicates salt or oil deposits beneath the surface.

In recent years, scientists have improved the gravimeter and devised new tools for measuring gravity. As a result, they have made some startling new discoveries.

Scientists are now picking up slight changes in gravity every day. They assume that these are related to earth tides, which are much like the ocean tides. The earth tides are actually changes in the shape of the land masses of the earth, caused by the gravitational pull of the sun and moon.

Gravity Waves

In 1915 in his theory of relativity, Albert Einstein suggested that gravity travels through space as gravity waves, just as light travels through space as light waves. Over the years, a number of scientists have tried unsuccessfully to detect gravity waves.

The first evidence of gravity waves was presented to a scientific meeting by Dr. Joseph H. Taylor of the University of Massachusetts in December 1978. For four years, Dr. Taylor headed a team that had been receiving radio signals from a pulsar, a star sending out short pulses of radio waves. By studying these radio signals, Dr. Taylor came to realize that the pulsar was circling another massive object in space at the rate of one complete orbit in just under eight hours.

According to Einstein's theory, the pulsar and the invisible object should have been sending out powerful gravity waves. As a result, they should have been losing speed, and slowing down as they traveled around each other. By means of Einstein's equations, Dr. Taylor calculated that it should have taken the pulsar 1/10,000th of a second longer every year to make one complete circle.

The radio signals coming from the pulsar were very regular. They allowed Dr. Taylor to make very precise measurements of its speed. Over the four years he was making observations, the pulsar slowed down 4/10,000ths of a second. This outcome fit exactly the figure based on Einstein's equation!

Since Dr. Taylor did not detect or observe gravity waves, this is only an indirect proof. Yet most experts agree that his findings are very strong evidence of the presence of gravity waves.

In 1979, several scientists around the world started major research projects to try to make direct observations of gravity waves. Experimenters at the University of Rochester and in Moscow are using a disk of sapphire crystal that they hope will be set into vibration by the passage of a gravity wave. Scientists at the Massachusetts Institute of Technology reflect a laser beam between mirrors to see if gravity waves will cause any change in the beam's position. The Jet Propulsion Laboratory in California has sent sensitive measuring instruments up into space to search for gravity waves. And in Australia and Italy, scientists are trying to find gravity waves by observing their effect on an aluminum cylinder kept at a very low temperature.

It has been said that we know more about space than we know about the earth's interior. Space shots enable us to make direct observations of conditions in space. But as yet, we can only gather information indirectly about the earth's "inner space." In this way, though, we are increasing our knowledge about the materials, conditions, and forces inside planet earth.

THE
CHANGING EARTH

THE EARTH'S CRUST IS always changing. It is gradually worn down by the forces of weathering and erosion. It is also slowly lifted upward, dropped downward, and moved sideways by powerful forces from within the earth.

Slow shifts of the earth's crust shape the continents. Sudden shifts cause powerful earthquakes. Islands rise up when volcanoes erupt and lava pours out from inside the oceanic crust. Mountain ranges form when the crust of the earth crumples up into uneven layers.

Drifting Continents

The idea that entire continents might be drifting and moving developed into a true science called plate tectonics around the year 1970. "Plate" refers to the giant jigsawlike plates that make up the earth's outer layer. "Tectonics" means building or construction. The scientists in this field study the plates themselves, and how they move and change. Plate tectonics is considered the most important new idea in earth science in the last 200 years.

According to the theory of plate tectonics, the entire outer layer of the earth is made up of about twelve giant plates. They are irregular in shape, millions of square miles in area, and about 40 to 50 miles (64 to 80 km) thick. They are like immense rafts slowly floating over the earth's mantle. And on their backs these plates carry the continents and oceans that make up the surface of the earth.

Although the plates fit into each other like pieces in a giant jigsaw puzzle, each of the plates is always moving. They move only tiny distances—maybe an inch or two a year. They move so slowly that no one can see or feel them moving. But changes in the face of the earth prove that they do move.

Scientists now believe that at some time in the distant past, all the continents on earth were joined into one immense single land mass. They call this supercontinent Pangaea, which means "all lands."

About 200 million years ago, when the dinosaurs were just beginning to appear on earth, Pangaea began to split apart.

The first split separated an immense northern continent from two smaller southern continents. Then about 30 million years later, the northern continent also broke into two separate continents.

Slowly, only inches at a time, these land masses drifted apart. A new layer of solid rock formed in the gaps left by the moving continents. In time, water filled in the space between the land we now call Europe and the land we now call North America. It became the Atlantic Ocean. The continents have been slowly drifting apart all these years and are still moving away from each other, a matter of inches every year.

Scientists have been developing an excellent new way to measure continental drift. In 1976, a satellite was placed in orbit 3,600 miles (5,800 km) above earth. It looks like a giant brass golf ball, covered with 426 small reflectors. Scientists aim high-powered pulses of laser light at the satellite. They measure the time it takes to be reflected back. In that way they can calculate the exact distance to the satellite.

Now laser guns are being positioned around the world, on various plates. The scientists will soon be able to track the exact rate and direction of the plates as they move about.

Even though scientists can measure the drift of the continents today, how can they prove that there ever was a single continent, Pangaea? There are some good clues.

Look at a map of the world. Do you see how Brazil and the rest of South America fit into the coastline of Africa? Do you see how the bulge of northern Africa follows the same line as the Atlantic coast of North America? Do you see how

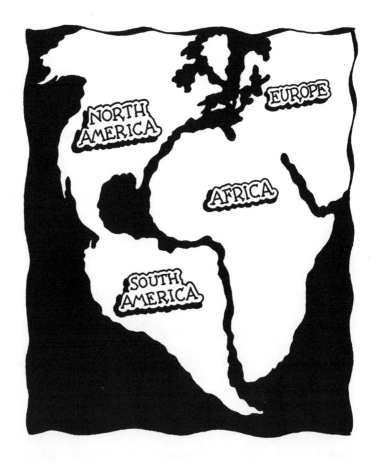

Canada, Greenland, and northern Europe could easily be fit together into one vast land mass?

It really looks as if all these lands are pieces of a giant jigsaw puzzle. And if you were to look at the continental shelf—the underwater edge of all the continents—you would see that the fit is even better. In the past, they all fit in together. Now they are apart—and still spreading.

Another clue is that there are similar rock formations in

areas on both sides of the Atlantic Ocean. The rocks found on Africa's Ivory Coast and in Brazil, in Scotland and in Labrador, and on the African island of Madagascar and in India are alike. Since the rocks in these widely separated areas are the same, it probably means that at some time in the past these places were joined together.

Still another clue is found in fossils found on both sides of the Atlantic. For example, in Brazil and Africa there are fossils of the same ancient fern that no longer exists. Remains of one type of snail, likewise extinct, are found both in Europe and North America. It is unlikely that the same ferns and snails developed in both places and then became extinct. So this is taken as further proof of continental drift.

Major changes in temperature in various areas of the world is further evidence of continental drift. For example, coal has been found in Antarctica, which indicates that warm-climate trees and plants once grew there; fossils of trees have been found in northern Norway, where no trees grow today. Perhaps these changes in climate were caused by land movement from warmer to colder spots on the globe.

These clues, though, raise an important question: What forces push the continents and make them drift apart?

The answer was found in the broad underwater mountain ranges. These mountains stretch for some 47,000 miles (75,000 km) under the oceans of earth. They are called midocean ridges. The Mid-Atlantic Ridge is in the middle of the Atlantic Ocean. Its north–south path is roughly parallel to the coasts on both sides of the Atlantic.

The most interesting feature of the Mid-Atlantic Ridge is the giant crack that runs along the top of the ridge. This crack, called a rift valley, is from 7 to 30 miles (11 to 48 km) wide and reaches to a depth of nearly 1 mile (1.6 km).

It is now believed that hot molten magma is forced up through the rift by the heat and pressure within the earth. The magma runs down the two sides of the slopes of the ridge. As the magma cools and becomes rock it becomes part of the plates on both sides of the ridge. The plates move and spread out. They move away from the ridge at the rate of about an inch (25 mm) a year.

Evidence that new rock is being created at the Mid-Atlantic Ridge is found by comparing rocks from the ocean floor and rocks from the continents. The oldest rocks ever found on the ocean floor are only 150 million years old. Yet the oldest rocks found on land are over 3,500 million years old. And on the ocean floor, rocks collected near the ridge were found to be no older than 1 million years. The farther away the rocks were found, though, the older they were, to a maximum of about 150 million years at the greatest distances from the ridge.

Earthquakes

Before plate tectonics, people had some strange ideas about the cause of earthquakes. In primitive times, people believed that angry gods or fights among the dead and buried were the cause. As science advanced, it was learned that quakes (short for earthquakes) are caused by large land masses moving and sliding past each other. But it was only in the last few years that they found that while some plates are drifting apart, other plates are pressing against each other. Then they realized that quakes occur when two plates rub together and then break free and slide past each other.

The North American plate and the Caribbean plate, for example, have been pushing against each other for the last 200 years or so. Over the years the pressure grew stronger and stronger. Then, on the morning of February 4, 1976, the Caribbean plate broke free. It jerked forward some 3 feet (1 m) along the North American plate.

The sudden movement shook the capital city of Guatemala City in Central America. The earth trembled and rocked. The streets cracked open, houses and other buildings collapsed. Fires blazed all over the city. In a few minutes, the earth stopped shaking. By the time it was all over, 70,000 people were injured, 20,000 were dead, and about 1 million were left homeless.

Nine out of every ten quakes take place along the borders between the plates, which are called faults. The most famous fault is the San Andreas fault that runs north and south near the California coast. The San Andreas fault is the border between the North American plate and the Pacific plate. The Pacific plate is moving toward the northwest in relation to the North American plate. Each time the plates break free of each other and suddenly shift, there is an earthquake. There have been at least thirty-five major quakes along the San Andreas fault over the last 150 years.

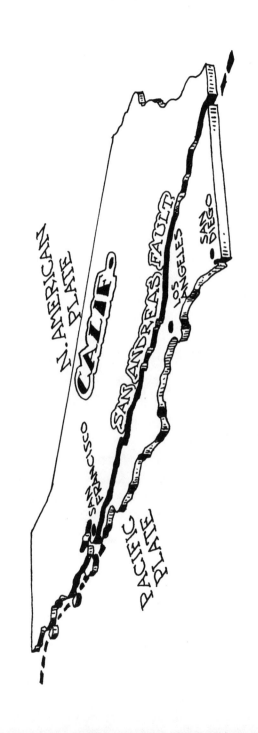

The worst one of all was the famous San Francisco earthquake of 1906.

Large faults can be many hundreds of miles long. Each quake, though, takes place along a short section of the fault, only a few miles long. The central point of origin of the quake is called the focus. The focus of almost every quake is beneath the surface of the earth, down to a depth of about 400 miles (643 km). The epicenter of the quake is the point on the surface, just above the focus.

When an earthquake occurs, immense amounts of energy are released from the focus. Waves of energy pour out in all directions through the earth. By receiving and measuring the different types of waves coming from the focus, scientists can tell the site of the quake, the time it occurred, and the strength of its waves.

The waves from a quake are received and measured on an instrument called a seismograph. It is based on a simple principle. An upright rod is firmly anchored on bedrock. A heavy weight hangs by a spring from the rod. During a quake the bedrock and rod vibrate, but because of inertia, the heavy weight remains stationary. A measure of the movement of the rod, in relation to the weight, is a measure of the quake.

The strength of earthquakes is usually described in terms of a Richter scale. On the Richter scale, a measurement of 1 is a very mild quake; 10 is the most violent. The strongest quake ever recorded in recent times reached an 8.6 on the Richter scale. Anything over 7 is a very destructive quake.

Earthquakes may occur anywhere on earth. Most,

though, take place along faults, where there is a great deal of pushing and shoving of the two bordering plates. The two most active earthquake zones are a giant ring around the Pacific Ocean and along the northern border of the Mediterranean Sea. About 80 percent of all quakes occur in the ring around the Pacific; about 15 percent along the Mediterranean region. Many of the remaining 5 percent occur along the midocean ridges. All of these are places where plates are rubbing against each other.

In recent years, scientists who study earthquakes have become more successful in predicting the occurrence of earthquakes. In 1975, they predicted a 7.4 Richter quake in Liaoning Province in China one month, and then one and one-half hours before it struck.

To predict an earthquake, scientists set sensitive measuring instruments on the ground to detect any changes in the tilt of the land. These laser devices can record differences as tiny as 1/50th of an inch (.05 cm) in 3 miles (4.8 km). When plates press against each other, the strain on the bedrock increases. The cracks already in the rock swell and expand, which leads to the increased tilt of the land.

Seismographs are used to keep a close record of the pattern of tiny miniquakes in an area. The miniquakes relieve the pressure of the plates. When they cease, it means the pressure is building up and a major quake is likely to occur.

Scientists have learned that an increased amount of radon, a radioactive substance, in deep well water can be an indicator of an approaching quake. The radon probably comes from rocks that are split open by the pressure before the quake, releasing radioactive gases.

Pet, farm, and zoo animals also offer clues to an approaching quake. For some unknown reason, many animals change their behavior before a quake strikes. They become very active and tense. Careful observation of animals, therefore, is helpful in making earthquake predictions.

Scientists around the world are finding that the water level in deep wells drops before a quake. In November 1978, Russian experts used this method to give six-hour warning of a quake in the Altai Mountains of central Asia.

In addition, scientists are studying the speed with which earthquake waves pass through the rock, changes in the magnetic field, and other factors that might help them to predict quakes. They are eager to become skilled at both short-term and long-term predictions. Long-term predictions would lead to warnings about areas where quakes can be expected. People could pass laws about building earthquake-proof structures in those areas. Short-term predictions would lead to plans for evacuation from endangered areas. It would help to prepare disaster relief forces.

A research project on preventing and controlling earthquakes was conducted at the Rangely Oil Field in Colorado from 1968 through 1973. The area had an average of twenty-eight mild quakes per month at the start of the study. Researchers decided that the heavy quake activity came from the high-pressure injections of water into the ground to flush out the oil. They tried to pump great amounts of water up out of the earth. They wanted to see if reduced pressure would cut the number of earthquakes.

The experiment was a great success. At the end, only one mild quake occurred per month. But the cost was so high that it made the method impractical. To reduce the underground pressure along the San Andreas fault in California, for example, would cost at least $50 million. For this reason, most researchers are now working on improved prediction, rather than on control.

Volcanoes

Beneath certain areas of the earth's surface, there is molten rock, or magma. If there is any break or opening in the crust, the magma may force its way up to the earth's surface. The opening, or conduit, through which the magma comes out is called a volcano.

Here is an experiment to show how minerals can expand and force their way to the surface. You will need plaster of paris, a paper cup, crayons, and a twelve-inch (30.5 cm) length of knitting yarn. Mix enough plaster of paris to fill a paper cup. Break a crayon into three equal pieces and tie a four-inch (10 cm) length of knitting yarn to each crayon bit. Holding one end of the yarn, push each crayon piece into the wet plaster so that it is away from the other pieces, and away from the sides or bottom of the cup. Let the yarn hang out over the top of the cup.

Put the cup aside until the plaster hardens. Tear the paper

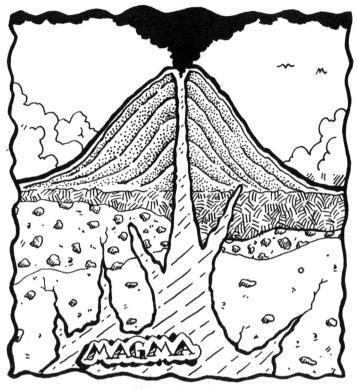

Volcano interior

cup away, and cut the yarn at the surface of the plaster. Place the hardened plaster over an open flame. Leave it on the flame while the crayon melts inside.

The crayon is like the molten rock under the surface of the earth. The lengths of yarn make tunnels in the plaster, similar to the conduits in the earth's crust. When the minerals (crayons) melt and expand, they squeeze out along the conduits (yarn tunnels), forming volcanoes.

The magma emerges through the conduit as lava. The

molten lava is usually between 1000° F and 2000° F (550° C and 1100° C). Sometimes the lava flows out quietly. Other times, great amounts of steam and other gases mixed in with the rock cause an explosive blast.

Along with the lava great amounts of smoke, ash, cinders, and rock are sometimes flung out of the volcano. The lava piles up, higher and higher, on all sides, and the volcano grows larger.

The world's largest volcano, Mauna Loa in Hawaii, has a quiet eruption about once every eight years. The lava flows out as a great river, perhaps one mile (1.6 km) wide and 40 miles (64 km) long. After about 1 million years of Mauna Loa's activity, the base of the volcano on the bottom of the Pacific Ocean has an area of nearly 13,000 square miles (34,000 sq. km). The top of the volcano reaches 6 miles (10 km) above the ocean floor.

On the morning of November 13, 1963, fishing boats were out in the waters around the North Atlantic island of Iceland. An immense black cloud suddenly burst up out of the water. A powerful wave radiated out, rocking the boats. Dust and pieces of lava rained down as the fishermen sped to leave the area of this erupting volcano.

All day long, smoke and lava were flung very high up into the air. By the following morning, a mountain that reached a full 30 feet (9 m) above the water had been created. After about two years, it had risen to a height of 500 feet (152 m). At its base, it covered an area of about 1 square mile (2.6 sq. km). By then the volcanic activity had stopped. Plants

Birth of an island

started to grow in the dirt that blew into the spaces around the lava. A completely new island, called Surtsey, had been formed.

Surtsey was created outside the two great volcano belts around the earth. The volcano belts are almost exactly the same as the earthquake areas.

The biggest volcano belt is called the Ring of Fire. It forms an irregular circle all around the Pacific Ocean, from the western coast of the United States to Alaska, across the Aleutian Islands, down Japan and the Philippines, across to New Zealand, and then up the western coasts of South and Central America. The other smaller belt stretches across the northern edge of the Mediterranean Sea. Mounts Etna and Vesuvius are two famous volcanoes in the Mediterranean belt. Volcanoes, like earthquakes, are found along the edges of the earth's plates.

Where plates meet and push against each other, one plate sometimes slips under the other. The plate that is pushed under goes down into the earth, usually at an angle of about $45°$.

As this plate is slowly forced down, it gets hotter and hotter because of the natural heat within the earth. Over millions of years, it reaches a depth of about 60 to 450 miles (97 to 724 km). The heat at this level is great enough to melt some of the rock of the plate.

This melted rock becomes part of the pool of magma. Most of it, in time, forms new igneous rocks. But some of this magma explodes through the surface as a volcano.

Recently, new ways have been found to predict when a volcano is about to erupt. Volcanic eruptions often follow a series of small earthquakes near the site of a volcano. Each of these quakes is closer to the surface than the one before. The actual volcanic eruptions seem to come after the quake that is nearest to the surface. This method was most successfully applied when a scientist predicted the exact day of a volcanic eruption in the New Hebrides Islands on November 3, 1963.

Scientists are also using new, sensitive instruments to measure and record any changes in the earth to help them predict volcanic eruptions. They use special thermometers to measure temperature changes in pools of lava. They send up satellites with equipment to measure heat flow below the surface of the earth. And they set out the delicate instruments used to record any tilting or bulging of the surface of the earth near volcanoes.

Mountain Building

The formation of mountains is also explained by plate tectonics. Earthquakes occur because the earth's plates slip, slide, and grind past each other. Volcanoes erupt along the edges of the earth's plates. And now scientists also believe that mountains form in places where the pressure between two plates is so great that it forces the rock of one or both plates to buckle up along the edges.

Here is a simple activity that will give you an idea of how mountains are formed. Place a heavy bath towel on a flat table or a smooth floor. Press the palms of both your hands

down on the towel, about a foot apart. Now slowly bring your hands together. Do you see how the towel forms ridges and folds between your hands?

The movement of your hands is like the pressure of the two plates against each other. The tiny mountains that form in the towel are like the real mountains that are created as the rocks give way to the power of the moving plates.

Scientists have long been struck by certain facts about mountains. Every great mountain range contains sedimentary rocks, rocks that were formed under the ocean. Fossils of ancient sea creatures are often found high up on mountains, thousands of feet above sea level. Also, most of the world's great mountain ranges are along the borders of the continents and roughly follow the same outline.

The science of plate tectonics helps to explain these related facts. Sedimentary rocks are found on mountains, and mountains are found along continental coasts because many coastlines correspond to the edges of plates where the land has been forced up.

The Alps of Europe were formed as the African plate and

the plate containing most of Europe and Asia pushed against each other. Under the tremendous pressure of these slow-moving, powerful plates, the earth buckled and folded and was gradually pushed up into towering peaks. Before the two plates collided, though, there was an ocean between them. What was once seabed, with its sedimentary rock and sea animal fossils, was slowly forced up to the mountain heights.

The pressure of the plate carrying India against the plate carrying the continent of Asia resulted in the formation of the world's tallest mountains, the Himalayas. This process is still going on as India continues to force its way northward. And in the Western Hemisphere, the Rockies of western United States and Canada, the Appalachians of the East, and the Andes in South America are all also believed to be the result of the pressure of one plate against another.

The great pressures in the earth shape the continents, cause earthquakes, and crack the crust so that volcanoes erupt. These same pressures create mountains. Drifting continents, earthquakes, volcanoes, and mountain formation are all ways in which the earth is constantly changing and evolving.

THE
BLANKET OF AIR

THE ATMOSPHERE IS AN INVISIBLE blanket of air
that completely surrounds our planet. It makes life on earth
possible. Almost every animal and plant needs air in order
to live. The atmosphere protects us from the harmful rays
and particles that strike earth from outer space. It keeps us
from burning up in the full heat of the sun during the day.
At night, it holds in the heat so that we do not freeze from
the cold. All the weather, including the rain and snow that
provide the earth with water, is found within the lower levels
of the atmosphere.

Layers of the Atmosphere

The air is thickest at the earth's surface. Here the molecules of the gases that make up the air are squeezed together by the weight of the air above them. The greater the distance from the earth's surface, the more space between the gas molecules and the thinner the air.

Nobody knows exactly how high the atmosphere stretches. Some scientists set the limit at about 18,000 miles (29,000 km). Above this level the gas molecules are so far apart that there is a vacuum. Here, too, the pull of the earth's gravity is so weak that the scattered molecules do not move through space with earth.

Scientists generally think of the atmosphere as being in five layers. The lowest layer is known as the troposphere. The name comes from a Greek word that means "turning" or "changing." It refers to the changing weather—the clouds, winds, storms, rain—in this layer. About 80 percent of the air in the atmosphere is found in the troposphere.

The higher you go in the troposphere, the colder it gets. At a certain level, between 5 miles (9 km) over the poles, and 10 miles (16 km) over the equator, the temperature no longer drops. This level is called the tropopause. It is the upper boundary of the troposphere. Temperatures in the tropopause range from about $-55°$ F to $-100°$ F ($-48°$ C to $-73°$ C).

The second level of the atmosphere is the stratosphere. The name comes from the Latin word for layer. The strato-

sphere is a quiet level, with none of the weather disturbances of the troposphere. Airplane pilots prefer to fly in the stratosphere because the thinner air offers less resistance to their planes and here they avoid the storms and winds of the lower levels. From bottom to top, the temperature of this region gradually rises until it reaches the stratopause at about 100° F (38° C). The stratopause is about 30 miles (48 km) above the surface of the earth. Temperatures do not rise beyond it.

The third layer, the mesosphere, reaches from the stratopause up about 50 miles (80 km) above the earth. The temperature pattern changes again. It drops steadily in this layer until it reaches a level known as the mesopause. The temperature is lower at the mesopause, about −135° F (−93° C), than anywhere else in the atmosphere. The mesopause also marks another change in temperature pattern. At this height, the temperature stops dropping.

This marks the beginning of the fourth layer of the atmosphere, the thermosphere. The thermosphere extends from the mesopause off into space. This is a region of steadily rising temperature. Here, though, the air is so thin that objects passing through the thermosphere are not warmed by the air.

The layer of air from about 40 to 300 miles (64 to 480 km) above the earth's surface is also called the ionosphere. Ions are atoms or molecules with electrical charges. Cosmic rays from space strike the atoms and molecules here, creating ions. The ionosphere makes radio broadcasting possible. The layer bounces back or reflects the signals sent out from radio stations. Without the ionosphere, the signals would head straight out into space, and could only be picked up on radio receivers that are in sight of the radio transmitter.

Above the thermosphere and the ionosphere is the exosphere. It reaches up to about 18,000 miles (29,000 km) above the earth. The distance between molecules is so great in the exosphere that some scientists say that each one is like a single Ping-Pong ball bouncing around in an empty gymnasium.

What Is Air?

Air is a mixture of many invisible gases. The most important ones are nitrogen (78 percent) and oxygen (21 percent). The remaining 1 percent is made up mostly of argon, carbon dioxide, neon, helium, krypton, xenon, hydrogen, and nitrous oxide.

The following experiment will show you that about 20 percent of the air is oxygen. You will need a candle, a large glass or wide-mouthed jar, and a flat pan.

Place the candle on the pan. Cover the bottom of the pan with about one-half inch (1.2 cm) of water. Light the candle and invert the glass or jar over it. The burning candle uses the oxygen of the air trapped inside the glass or jar in order to burn. As the candle uses up the oxygen, the water rises in the glass to take its place. Soon the candle uses up all the oxygen, and the flame goes out.

Measure the height that the water rose in the jar. Divide this height by the total height of the jar. Multiply by 100 to get the percentage of oxygen in the air in the jar. This experiment shows you that about 20 percent of the air is oxygen.

The balance of gases in the air always stays the same, even though the actual molecules are continually changing. For example, when animals breathe, they remove oxygen from the air and release carbon dioxide. At the same time, plants remove carbon dioxide from the air and release oxygen, maintaining the oxygen balance. In a similar way, nitrogen is removed from the air by bacteria in the soil and in the roots of certain plants. When the plants die, or when animals that eat the plants die, the nitrogen is returned to the air.

The carbon dioxide in the air allows the sun's rays through to heat the earth's surface. But it does not let the heat waves escape from the surface of the earth. It traps the earth's heat, gradually building up the temperature. Since this is the same sort of thing that happens in a greenhouse, it is called the greenhouse effect.

Some scientists now fear that more and more carbon dioxide is entering the atmosphere as we continue burning fuels like oil and coal. They also point out that as we cut down more forests, we lose the benefit of the trees and plants that take in carbon dioxide and produce oxygen, and add even more carbon dioxide to the atmosphere. Because of the greenhouse effect we may therefore be raising the earth's temperature and may be in danger of melting the ice at the North and South poles—which could completely change the conditions on earth.

Air Pressure

The gases that make up the atmosphere are held in place by the earth's gravity. Gravity pulls the gases of the atmosphere toward the center of the earth. The mass of air over every square inch of the earth's surface, pulled down by the earth's gravity, weighs 14.7 pounds (6.68 kg). The weight is known as air pressure.

To prove that air has weight, get two identical balloons. Blow one up and tie a knot to keep it closed. Leave the other one as it is. Use a balance or a delicate scale to compare the weights of the balloons. You will find that the blown-up balloon weighs more because of the weight of the air it contains.

You don't feel air pressure most of the time because it is the same both inside and outside your body. But air pressure decreases very rapidly as you go higher. When you rise quickly in an elevator or on a mountain road, the sudden drop in pressure makes your ears "pop."

Air pressure is related to temperature. To see how temperature changes air pressure, obtain two balloons and two small bottles. Fit a balloon around the top of each bottle and set the bottles into two deep pans. Fill one pan with ice and the other with hot water.

Notice how one balloon inflates and expands, while the other does not inflate at all. The hot water warms the air in one bottle. The air expands beyond the bottle and inflates the balloon. The ice in the other pan cools the air in the bottle. The air contracts, and none of it goes into the other balloon.

We use air pressure all the time. For example, when we breathe in, the air pressure in our chests is reduced. This causes outside air, at the normal pressure, to rush in. When we breathe out, the pressure is increased. Also, to drink through a straw, you reduce the air pressure in your mouth. The pressure on the surface of the liquid forces it up through the straw.

Air does not only press down. It presses sideways and upward as well. This experiment will prove to you that air presses in all directions.

Fill a glass to the top with water. Cover the glass with a piece of cardboard. Slowly and carefully, holding the cardboard in place, turn the glass to one side over a sink. Then let go of the cardboard.

Why does the cardboard stay in place, even though you are not holding it? It stays in place because the sideways pressure of the air holds it there. Next hold the glass upside down. The air pressure pressing up on the cardboard is strong enough to keep the cardboard in place, despite the weight of the water in the glass.

Air Movement

Most of the earth's heat that we feel comes from the surface of the earth, which is warmed by the sun. Just as a candle feels cooler a foot above the flame than an inch above the flame, so the higher you get the less you feel the heat from the earth's surface.

The temperature of the air drops about 3 1/2° F (2° C) for every 1,000 feet (305 m) above sea level. If the temperature at sea level is 75° F (24° C), the temperature on top of a 1,000 foot (1,600 km) mountain is 71.5° F (22° C); on top of a 10,000 foot (16,000 km) mountain, 40° F (4.4° C); and on top of Mount Everest, 29,000 feet (46,660 km) high, −27° F (−32.7° C).

When air is warmed, it expands and becomes lighter. Therefore, warmer air rises, and cooler, heavier air moves in to replace it. This movement of air causes winds.

You can create an air movement, or wind, in this simple experiment. All you need is a piece of thick twine, a match, and a source of heat, such as a radiator or a turned-on light bulb.

Light the end of the twine with the match to create some smoke. Hold it over the source of heat. See how the warm

air carries the smoke up. In a room that is heated by a radiator, the warm air rises. The cool air falls and moves in to take its place. Around and around the air moves like a very gentle wind.

The heated air around the equator is always rising. Colder air at the poles creates regions of high pressure. Since air tends to move from high toward low pressures, there is a general flow of air, or wind, from the poles toward the equator near the earth's surface. At higher levels, there is a return flow of warm air from the equator toward the poles.

Air Pollution

Natural winds mix the air and maintain its normal composition. But every day the balance is being upset by unwanted and undesirable gases and tiny bits of matter that are released into the atmosphere by people on earth. These irritating, often dangerous substances, called pollutants, create air pollution.

Most pollutants are produced when fires do not completely burn their fuel. Automobiles, power plants, factories, and home heating furnaces are the main sources of pollutants.

Americans add about 300 million tons of gas and solid pollutants to the air every year. Nearly 150 million tons are emitted by cars, trucks, and buses. Another 50 million tons pour out of furnaces that are used to generate electricity and to heat buildings; 40 million tons more originate from factories as the result of their production activities; 15 million tons result from the burning of garbage and other waste; and the final 45 million tons are derived from sources that range from forest fires to hair sprays.

Usually the air at the surface is warmer than the air higher up. The warm air rises and the cooler air drops to be warmed

and rise in turn. But from time to time the air in a particular area does not follow the normal patterns of air movement. Occasionally a mass of warm air forms over an area. It traps cooler air at the surface, which does not rise. When this occurs it is called a temperature inversion.

During a temperature inversion, the air masses do not move. The pollutants in the air are not carried away. People are sickened or even killed. Plants wither and may perhaps die. A pollution emergency is a dangerous situation. It can only be controlled by ceasing all activities that add pollutants to the air until the weather changes and the air begins to circulate again.

Since our very life depends on a clean, pure atmosphere, any threat to the balance of elements in the atmosphere is a threat to the existence of living things on this planet.

OCEANS, LAKES, AND RIVERS

NEARLY 75 PERCENT OF the earth's surface, about 140 million square miles (360 million sq. km), is covered with water. This includes oceans, lakes, rivers, bays, and gulfs. The part of the earth that is covered by water is known as the hydrosphere.

Most of the earth's water is found in the great oceans of the world. The continents divide these bodies of water into the Pacific, Atlantic, Indian, and Arctic oceans. These are not, though, separate bodies of water. They are connected and really form one large body of water.

The Water Cycle

You know that water evaporates. Unless it is kept in a sealed container, water slowly and gradually disappears. Actually, the water just changes its state. It goes from a liquid, which you can see and feel, to water vapor, which is an invisible gas. The water vapor mixes in with the surrounding air. Humidity is a measure of the amount of water vapor in the air. As much as 5 percent of the air can be water vapor on a day when the humidity is high.

Great amounts of water are always evaporating from the hydrosphere. The water vapor becomes part of the warmer air near the earth's surface. This warmer air, being lighter than cold air, tends to rise. It rises to colder and colder levels.

When it reaches a cold enough level, the water vapor changes its state. It forms little drops of liquid water in a process called condensation.

The condensation occurs because warm air can hold more water vapor than cold. When you exhale on a cold day, the water vapor in your warm breath condenses in the cool air and forms a mist of tiny drops of water. When the water vapor from a hot bath touches the cold window or mirror in the bathroom, drops of water form on these surfaces because of condensation.

The water vapor that condenses in the air then falls to earth as drops of rain. If it is cold enough, the water freezes and falls as snow, hail, or sleet. This replaces the water that evaporated. The amount of water on earth, therefore, stays the same throughout time. This movement of water through evaporation and condensation is called the water cycle.

Composition of Ocean Waters

The chemical formula for water, H_2O, means that two atoms of hydrogen are joined with one atom of oxygen to form each molecule of water. Yet when 1,000 pounds (454 kg) of ocean water are evaporated, about 35 pounds (16 kg) of solids remain. The solids are mostly mineral salts, largely sodium chloride, or common table salt. These solids make ocean water salt water.

Earth scientists believe that the first water on earth was sweet and not salty. It formed into rivers and streams that flowed into the oceans. The rivers dissolved mineral salts in the rocks over which they flowed and brought them to the seas.

The sweet water part of ocean water is always evaporating. Therefore the remaining water becomes even saltier. The fact that the earth's oceans are steadily getting saltier is evidence that the waters were originally sweet. The two saltiest bodies of water in the world are the Dead Sea in Israel and the Great Salt Lake in Utah. The Dead Sea is in a very warm area, which speeds up evaporation and increases the percentage of salt in the water. The water of the Great Salt Lake does not drain out. It slowly evaporates, leaving the salt.

If you live near an ocean, you can make your own salt. Collect some ocean water in a clean, wide-mouthed bottle. Set the bottle, without a cover, in a warm, clean place. In a few days, the sweet water will evaporate. Left on the bottom of the bottle will be a layer of white or gray powder. That is the salt. Wet a finger, touch the salt, and taste it. Do you get a salty taste? Some people believe that salt obtained from ocean water is healthier and more nutritious than common table salt.

In addition to salt, two other chemicals, magnesium and bromine, are obtained from sea water. Magnesium is a metal used in the construction of airplanes. Bromine is used for photography and in the manufacture of gasoline.

A good deal of air is dissolved in most water. You can see this for yourself. Fill a tall glass with cold water. Put it on a warm radiator or stove and heat it gently. What happens?

The bubbles that appear on the sides are made by the air that was dissolved in the water.

In areas of the Pacific, Atlantic, and Indian oceans, the seafloor is covered with potato-sized lumps of metal, called nodules. They are made up mostly of the metal manganese, which is very important in the manufacture of steel. In addition, these nodules contain amounts of cobalt, copper, and nickel, as well as some other metals. Some of them are being dredged up on an experimental basis as engineers try to develop economic methods of mining these metals from the seafloor.

The most important resource found in, or rather under, the oceans is oil. Some geologists estimate that there is more oil under the continental shelves around the world's continents than there is under the land of the continents. Special oil platforms are placed at sea to drill for this oil.

Waves and Currents

Waves are caused by the wind. If you blow gently across the surface of a pan of still water, you will see ripples form. Notice that the ripples stop when you stop blowing. The wind, though, blows on the sea longer and harder, making larger waves that continue after the wind has stopped blowing. They have enough energy to keep traveling hundreds of miles across the ocean. That is why you can see waves even on a windless day.

Waves are constantly at work. They break rock into boulders, pebbles, and sand. When the waves break on a beach they push sand, shells, and gravel up on the beach. As the water runs back, it drags sediment into the sea. The pounding of waves is always changing the shoreline.

Sometimes earthquakes set huge waves in motion. These waves may move several hundred miles an hour. They are called tsunamis, or tidal waves. A typical tsunami has a length of 90 miles (145 km) and a speed of about 450 miles (724 km) per hour. Waves of this kind can be very destructive.

Ocean waves are a potential source of energy. For example, the waves created by an average ocean liner carry ten times more power than is needed to drive the ship.

Waves move on the surface of the ocean. Currents are rivers of moving water within the ocean. The earth's rotation makes the currents move. They flow clockwise in the Northern Hemisphere, counterclockwise in the Southern Hemisphere. You can see the effect of the earth's rotation the next time you take a bath or shower. Notice that the water always swirls in the same direction as it flows down the drain.

To see how rotation causes currents, you can also place a large bowl half full of water on a lazy Susan. Slowly turn the lazy Susan in one direction. Do you see a current set up in the water? Reverse the direction and notice the change in the direction of the current movement.

There are four main currents in the earth's oceans. The warm Gulf Stream flows from the Gulf of Mexico across the Atlantic Ocean to Great Britain, and then on to Iceland. The cold Labrador Current starts in the Arctic Ocean and flows into the North Atlantic where it meets the Gulf Stream. It sinks under the Gulf Stream and returns cold water to the tropical zones to be warmed and start its journey again.

The warm Japan Current circles all the way around the Pacific Ocean, reaching from Japan and the coast of Asia to the west coast of Canada and the United States. The warm Equatorial Currents run roughly parallel to the equator. The part just north of the equator runs from east to west and occasionally breaks off into a clockwise circle. The part south of the equator runs from west to east and joins counterclockwise current movements.

Scientists have long known of the ocean currents. But it is only in recent years that they have come to understand these "rivers" in the oceans. Their main research tool is the float.

The usual float is a long, hollow metal tube. Scientists add weights so that the float will remain at any desired depth. Inside, a battery-powered sounder sends out loud "pings," which can be heard over great distances.

The scientists throw floats into the currents from their research ships. With special underwater microphones they then listen to the pings as the floats are carried along by the current.

Several discoveries have been made about ocean currents in recent years. Most have pointed out the fact that currents are not simply rivers in the sea, as some had thought. Instead, they are highly complex systems, with many different directions and speeds within the overall flow.

Two discoveries have been made about countercurrents. These are currents, far underneath surface currents, that flow in the opposite direction. One was found about 700 feet (213 m) beneath the westward-flowing South Equatorial Current in the Pacific. It is flowing eastward at about 3 miles (5 km) an hour. Nine thousand feet (2,740 m) beneath the Gulf Stream is a countercurrent flowing south at about 8 miles (13 km) a day.

The currents contribute to the world's weather. The warm ones bring mild climates to the areas they touch. The cold ones do the opposite. England and Norway would have much colder climates without the warmth of the Gulf Stream. Labrador, which is on the same latitude, is chilled by the Labrador Current and has a much colder climate. The warm waters of the Gulf Stream keep the Russian port of Murmansk free of ice, even though it is north of the Arctic Circle.

While the currents affect the world's climate, the climate also affects the currents. In general, the surface currents carry warm water from the equator toward the poles. At the same time, deeper currents bring cooler water back toward the equator.

To find out how temperatures affect ocean currents, obtain two glass bottles with narrow necks. Fill one with cold water and the other with hot. Color the hot water with ink or food coloring.

Cover the mouth of the cold water bottle with a 3 by 5 inch index card. Carefully turn the bottle upside down, directly over the container of hot water. Slowly remove the card.

What do you observe? In what direction does the colored hot water flow? Why? Scientists hold that the heating of the ocean waters in the Gulf of Mexico creates the Gulf Stream. Cold water coming from the north forces warm water, which is lighter than cold water, upward and northward to form this great current.

The Ocean Floor

The oceans have an average depth of between 2 1/2 miles and 7 miles (4 and 11 km). Scientists measure the depth of the ocean by sonar, or echo sounding. They send short bursts

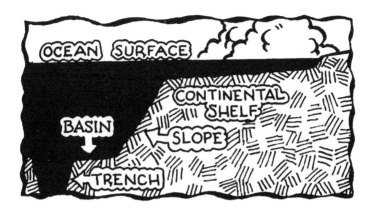

of high-pitched sound from the bottom of their ships toward the ocean floor. When the sound wave reaches the bottom it is echoed, or reflected back, to the ship. Sensitive instruments measure the time it takes for the sound to echo back. Since the speed at which sound travels through water is known, the instruments can then automatically calculate the depth of the water.

Surrounding the land masses of the world are gentle slopes called continental shelves. On an average, the continental shelves extend out about 40 miles (64 km) from the shoreline. At the end of the continental shelves, the depth of the water is about 400 feet (122 m), which is very deep for swimming, but very shallow compared to the rest of the ocean.

At the edge of the continental shelves, the seafloor abruptly drops downward. These stretches are called the continental slopes. The continental slopes extend out 10 and 20 miles (16 and 32 km) beyond the continental shelves. In this short distance, though, the seafloor drops from 400 to 12,000 feet (122 to 3,660 m).

At the end of the continental slopes is the basin, the true floor of the ocean. The basin is far from a flat expanse. Vast mountain ridges and volcanoes rise from the floor. Some come through the surface of the ocean and form islands. The midocean ridges make up a mountain range 47,000 miles (75,600 km) long. Deep cracks in the ocean basin are called trenches. The deepest one is the Marianas trench in the Pacific Ocean near Guam. It is over 36,000 feet (10,800 m) deep.

The ocean floor is covered with thick layers of sediment. Close to the continents, the sediment is made up mostly of gravel, sand, clay, and broken shells. Away from land, the sediment is mostly a soft ooze of microscopic sea animal shells and volcanic dust. Beneath the sediment is the bedrock of the ocean floor. It is made up largely of basalt, an igneous rock. The continents, on the other hand, rest on granite, also an igneous rock, but lighter than basalt.

By studying the layers in a sample of ocean sediment, scientists learn the history of the ocean. To scoop sediment from the ocean bottom they lower a hollow tube, called a core sampler, into the ocean. Above the tube are heavy weights that drive the tubing into the ocean floor. A sample of the ocean bottom is caught in the tube and brought up out of the water. Scientists then examine the layers of animal remains, volcanic dust, and other material to learn about the ocean's past.

Scientists are now studying seafloors down to 18,500 feet (5,500 m), beneath the layers of sediment. Cores from bedrock under the Atlantic and Pacific oceans are brought up and studied. The sediment is also being analyzed for clues to climate changes and their relationship to ocean currents, and to the origin of the oceans.

Water Pollution

Water pollution results when anything is added to water that does not normally belong there. When a tanker filled with oil springs a leak, it may spill thousands of gallons of thick, heavy oil into the water. The oil either poisons or kills the fish and sea animals, making them unfit to be eaten. The oil also forms a film on the water that keeps sunlight from reaching the plants. The plants die. Since the fish have less food to eat, soon there are fewer fish.

When a factory dumps chemical wastes into a river, the poisoned water may turn a fresh stream with living fish into a dead, smelly sewer. The polluted water may become part of the water supply of nearby cities and towns. Or it may flow into the sea and enter the bodies of fish. Then, when the fish are caught and eaten, the poisons enter the systems of other living beings.

When chemicals in detergents are dumped into bodies of water, they become extra food for certain plants that live there. These plants grow very fast and they crowd out other plants. Eventually the crowded-out plants die. As they decay, they use up the oxygen needed by the fish, and the fish die in great numbers.

There are many sources of water pollution, and once water is polluted it stays that way for a very long time. That is why there is no quick and easy way to clean up the earth's water. Our best hope is that no more pollution will be added. Then, over the years, the waters of the world may gradually be able to rid themselves of these dangerous substances.

LIFE ON EARTH

IT IS NOT POSSIBLE to count all the billions of plants and animals that live on earth today. They live on the land, in the waters, and in the air that you breathe. They range in size from tiny bacteria and viruses to the giant sequoia trees of California and the great whales. They are found miles above the earth's surface and in the depths of the oceans. They live in the frozen wilderness of the Arctic and in the tropical heat of the equator.

The biosphere is the zone around the earth where animals and plants can live. It includes the land surface, the water, and the lower levels of the atmosphere. The biosphere is only a very small part of the total earth. It has 1/300th the mass of the atmosphere and 1/40,000th the mass of the hydrosphere.

Origin of Life

Scientists believe that the earth was formed about 4.6 billion years ago. For more than 2 billion years there was no life of any kind on earth.

Then, about 2.3 billion years ago, several of the elements needed to support life began to appear. In 1953, the young scientist Stanley Miller was able to show how these lifeless elements might have become the first form of life.

In his experiment, Miller mixed together the gases believed to have been present during the early history of the earth. These included methane, ammonia, water vapor, and hydrogen. He kept them at the probable temperature of the earth in its early stages. Miller then sent electrical charges through the gases to duplicate the lightning and electrical storms that occurred on earth.

At the end of one week, Miller found that he had created several types of organic molecules. These organic molecules, Miller believed, were the basic building blocks of all forms of life on earth.

Miller and other scientists have gone on to show how these simple organic molecules could have combined to form more complex molecules, called proteins. In time, some of the proteins joined to form living systems that could grow and reproduce.

The first living beings were probably similar to today's bacteria and molds. For perhaps 1 billion years they were the only kind of life on earth.

Evolution of Life

Very slowly and gradually, changes took place in these living things. Over long periods of time, new forms of life developed. Most of the new types or species were more complex and efficient than the older forms. About 600 million years ago, the very earliest ancestors of a few of today's animal and plant species began to appear on earth.

Among the members of any species there is great variety. Some individuals are better able to survive. They may be bigger, stronger, or healthier. Perhaps they are better able to endure shortages of food or water, or extremes of climate. These individuals live on and pass along their helpful traits to their offspring.

There are also individuals with less successful characteristics. Often they die early and do not bear young. Therefore, they do not pass on their traits. In time, these less helpful traits disappear from the population. When an entire species is not fit for the environment, that species becomes extinct. This process is called natural selection.

About 30 to 40 million years ago, natural selection led to the appearance on earth of a completely new type of animal, the mammal. Mammals are warm-blooded animals, usually with hair, that feed milk to their young.

One line of mammals that started to develop included the ancestors of today's human beings. Until recently scientists believed that this line divided some 15 million years ago. One line, which developed long, powerful arms for living in trees, led to today's apes. The other line, which developed as upright ground animals, fit for walking, led to today's human beings.

The work of several scientists at the University of California at Berkeley has recently cast serious doubt that the split occurred 15 million years ago. By tracing differences and similarities between the different species, they have worked out a new timetable of each species' appearance on earth. According to their figures, the split between apes and humans did not occur until between 4 and 6 million years ago.

Another researcher, Adrienne Zihlman, at the University of California at Santa Cruz, agrees with their findings. But she has gone even further. She claims to have found the missing link, the animal from which both the apes and human are descended. The animal, now extinct, is very similar to today's pygmy chimpanzees that are found only in a small area of Zaire in equatorial Africa. The pygmy chimp moves as easily on the ground as in the trees. It does not have the long arms common to apes, and in brain size and arrangement of teeth it is more like humans than apes.

When did the first human being appear on earth? It is almost impossible to say. One of the oldest ancestors of modern man was discovered in 1959 in Tanganyika, Africa. Scientists found a human skull, a hand ax, and the fossil remains of a child that they estimated to be nearly 2 million years old. A few other so-called ape-men have been found in different places and are believed to be just as old.

These were accepted until recently as being the first people on earth. An important discovery in 1978 pushed the date back to more than 3 million years ago. A human footprint in volcanic ash was found in Africa. It had been covered over by lava, preventing erosion. The minerals in the lava show that it was about 3.5 million years old.

Study of the footprint shows that this first humanlike creature was about 4 feet (1.2 m) tall, walked very slowly, and took short steps. The foot size was short and very wide —about 6 inches (152 mm) long and 4 1/2 inches (114 mm) wide.

Most finds of early humans, though, date from about 1 million years ago. The well-known ones are Java man, Peking man, Neanderthal man, and Cro-Magnon man. Cro-Magnon man brings us up to the Stone Age, and the emergence of modern men and women.

Conditions for Life on Earth

Since the origin of life on earth, living things have multiplied and spread out over the entire surface of the world. They survive under varying conditions of temperature, humidity, soil, light, and air. But while they exist under almost all conditions, there are certain factors that must be present for life to go on.

Liquid water is most important. It is necessary in some amount for every living thing on earth. Animals need water in order to create the body fluids that transport food and oxygen to the cells and carry away wastes. All body fluids are principally water, with various elements and compounds in solution.

Water is also a protection. It absorbs and loses heat very slowly. These slow changes of temperature are necessary for the survival of plants and animals that live in the water.

When water freezes it forms ice, which is lighter than water and floats on ponds, lakes, and streams. Life continues beneath this layer. If the ice did not float and bodies of water froze from the bottom up, fish and sea animals could not survive.

Soil is basic for life. The plants that are the main food supply of animals get most of the elements and water they need through roots in the soil. Soil is also the home of numerous kinds of small animals. Dig up a potful of earth from outdoors and spread it out on a sheet of paper. How many ants, worms, beetles, slugs, and other animals can you find?

The soil supports billions of bacteria and other small creatures that are not easily seen. These tiny organisms play an important part in the decay process. The decay adds needed minerals to the soil, which helps growing plants. These plants can then provide food for animals. In time the animals die and start to decay, completing the cycle. This food cycle is vital for life on earth.

All green plants depend on light energy from the sun in order to grow. These plants, in turn, provide food for animals. Sometimes it is directly, as when humans eat vegetables or fruits, or indirectly, as when we eat meat from cattle that have eaten grass or other plants.

Almost all animals require oxygen for life. The oxygen is found either in the atmosphere or as a dissolved gas in water. Animals that live in the soil are most abundant near the surface, where the supply of oxygen is the greatest.

To find out what conditions are necessary for plant life, dig up a 6 inch × 6 inch (15 cm × 15 cm) square of grass-covered soil. Dig down deep enough to include the roots of the plants. Carefully divide the square into eight clumps of grass plants. Place each clump into a separate dish or bottom part of a cut-off milk container. Keep each specimen under different conditions:

Specimen 1   No light, but water
Specimen 2   No water, but light
Specimen 3   Neither light nor water
Specimen 4   No soil (shake off the soil from the roots), but light and water
Specimen 5   No air (place a plastic bag tightly over the grass plant, and seal it shut), but light, water, and soil
Specimen 6   Very hot, but light, water, soil, and air
Specimen 7   Very cold, but light, water, soil, and air
Specimen 8   Normal conditions of light, water, soil, air, and moderate temperature

Check the results of each specimen. What happens to each group of plants after one day? After three days?

The Biosphere and Man

For the most part, the earth has been kind to living things. Despite the advance and retreat of glaciers, changes in climate, shifts in continents, earthquakes, volcanoes, and other natural disasters, the earth has supported life and living things have flourished and multiplied.

People have changed conditions on earth, though. We have changed the composition of air by releasing poisonous fumes and dangerous chemicals into the atmosphere. Some of these chemicals may bring about long-term changes in the world's climate. By dumping various pollutants into the waters we have made much of the water unsafe to drink.

Many fish, birds, and other animals that live in or near bodies of water die every year. Chemicals and other wastes have seeped into soils. Poor agricultural practices have exhausted the soil. In many places the land has been stripped and the mineral wealth in the ground has been depleted. Pollution of the air, water, and land is making it increasingly difficult for life to exist on earth.

Fortunately many people are turning their attention to the dangers that face our planet earth and our life on it. What about you? Are you part of the effort to preserve the elements of the earth and to protect the things in the thin zone of life known as the biosphere?

HISTORY
OF THE EARTH

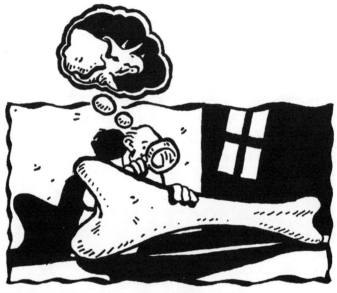

TO THE TRAINED SCIENTIST, the earth's rocks offer
a fascinating glimpse of the history of the earth. Rocks are
always changing. They are crumbled and broken by weathering. The smaller pieces of rock are carried away by erosion.
They are deposited by streams and rivers as sediment on the
seafloor and on lake bottoms. In time, these layers of sediment become sedimentary rock.

Meanwhile plants and animals are living and dying on the
land and in the water. As they die, their remains fall into the
sediment. When the sediment forms into rock, the animals
and plants are preserved as fossils.

At the same time, the great plates that make up the earth's surface are slowly and gradually moving, a tiny fraction of an inch at a time. Over thousands and millions of years, though, they change the surface of the earth. Bit by bit, old mountains, rivers, oceans, valleys, and plains disappear. New ones appear in different locations.

Then, all at once, a period of sudden change begins. Volcanoes erupt and earthquakes rip the earth apart. Immense mountains appear. Vast layers of rock are forced up into the air. Different patterns of weather and climate develop. Some of the old types of plant and animal life disappear, and new forms take their place.

This period of violent change is called a revolution. The revolutions are used to divide the earth's history into a number of eras and periods that stretch back nearly 5 billion years to the creation of the earth.

Five Eras of History

By careful study of the earth's rocks and the fossils they contain, the scientists who specialize in the history of the earth have divided the earth's history into five major eras.

The first two eras of the earth's history are known as the Archeozoic Era ("archeo" means beginning or primitive; "zoic" means life) and the Proterozoic ("earlier life") Era. The Archeozoic Era began with the formation of the earth about 4.6 billion years ago and lasted 3 billion years. The Proterozoic Era began some 1.6 billion years ago and lasted

1 billion years. The two eras are often considered together as the Precambrian Era. The 4 billion years of the Precambrian Era make up five-sixths of the entire history of the earth.

Scientists have found some fossils of very small sea plants and worms in rocks that date from late in the Archeozoic Era. Many more forms probably existed. But since these other plants and animals were without shells or bones, there are no fossil records of them. All of the fossils that do exist are of sea plants and animals. There is no evidence of life on land during this period.

Precambrian rocks show signs of a great deal of volcanic activity. Portions of the earth's crust melted and cooled many times. Melted rock was pushed up through the existing crust and hardened there.

The third era, the Paleozoic ("old life"), began 600 million years ago and lasted about 375 million years. Fossils of the first vertebrates (animals with backbones), the first insects, the first amphibians, the first reptiles, and the first land plants and animals are found in the rocks of this era. Many sea animals and plants appeared, developed, and died out in the Paleozoic Era.

A great variety of life developed on the vast flat areas that were flooded with shallow sea waters. Trees and plants grew in the swampy ground. Much later, coal formed from the remains of these trees and plants.

The Paleozoic Era ended with the so-called Appalachian revolution about 225 million years ago, when the Appala-

chian chain of mountains, stretching from Canada down along the Atlantic coast to Alabama, came into being. Several other mountain chains were formed at the same time. This era also saw the eruption of a great number of volcanoes and the melting of glaciers that had covered vast areas of land.

The Mesozoic ("middle life") Era began with the Appalachian revolution. It ended with the Laramide revolution, about 155 million years later, when the Rocky Mountains were formed.

Large numbers of animals developed during the Mesozoic Era. The very first mammals on earth appeared during this period. The earliest remains of dinosaurs also date from around the same time.

The first dinosaurs were comparatively small animals, about 15 feet (4.6 m) long. By the end of the era, however, they had become immense. One dinosaur was Tyrannosaurus Rex, which grew to be about 50 feet (15 m) long, stood 20 feet (6 m) high on its rear legs, and weighed several tons. Its teeth, about 6 inches (15 cm) long, were as sharp as razors.

The Cenozoic ("modern life") Era began with the Laramide revolution 70 million years ago. It still continues today. The Cenozoic is best known as the era of mammals. Mammals have become the dominant form of life on earth, climaxing in the appearance of the human species.

The land underwent many changes during the Cenozoic Era. The crust was lifted and mountains, such as the Alps and Himalayas, were raised. There was a major change in the climate as warm, humid conditions at the beginning of the era gave way to an ice age.

More and more water froze, causing sea levels to drop. Land bridges appeared between North America and Asia, and between North and South America. Glaciers covered vast areas of land. Over the next million years, these vast ice sheets formed and melted four times. They cut through mountains, eroded the land, and left large deposits of ground-up rock. When the glaciers of the ice age melted, rivers and lakes were formed.

The last ice age ended about 11,000 years ago. Many earth scientists believe that we are now in a warm period before another ice age. They say that the earth's climate is gradually growing colder. But another ice age is not an immediate threat. Historically the period between the formation of huge glaciers is over 100,000 years.

Dating the Past

Scientists use the revolutions for the approximate dates of the five major eras of the earth's history—Archeozoic, Proterozoic, Paleozoic, Mesozoic, and Cenozoic. But advances in earth science now permit even finer, more precise ways to date the earth's history.

The rate at which a stream or river erodes its bed is one way scientists measure geological time. Niagara Falls is the most famous example. Over the 200 years that scientists have been taking measurements, Niagara Falls has eroded the rocky ledge over which it passes at an average rate of 4 feet (1.2 m) a year. The gorge in front of the Falls is about 7 1/2 miles (12 km) long. By dividing the gorge length by the rate per year, they calculate that Niagara Falls is about 9,000 years old.

The rate of deposition is another way to date the past. It is known that it takes an average of about 7,000 years for a 1-foot (0.3 m) layer of sedimentary rock to form. A layer of sedimentary rock with a depth of, say, 20 feet (6 m) probably formed over a period of 140,000 years.

You can see how the scientist measures time with deposition in this experiment. Save the newspapers at your home. Place them in a neat pile, adding the new papers on top every day.

After four days, measure the height of the pile. Divide the total height by four to get the average height of each day's papers.

Continue collecting the papers for ten days. Again measure the total height of the pile. Is this figure about ten times the average height? Can you guess how high the pile will be in twenty days? If you saw another pile, could you figure out about how many papers it contained and how long they had been collected?

The newspapers in this experiment are like the layers of sedimentary rock deposited on earth. The earlier ones go down first, the later ones above them. By learning the average yearly rate of increase in height, it is possible to know the age of the rock at every level.

The layers of sediment deposited by a stream or a glacier help to fix geological dates in another way. The flow of water into a lake varies at different times of the year. When there is a rapid flow of water, or in the summer when a glacier is melting more rapidly, large amounts of sand, silt, and clay are carried into the lake. The heavier sand and silt particles quickly settle to the bottom. They form a layer that is light in color. The clay particles, which are lighter in weight than the other particles in the sediment, continue to float about in the water.

Then, when there is less flow, or when the lake is frozen over so that the winds do not stir the water, the clay particles settle out. They form a dark layer over the other lighter-colored layer. The two layers, making up one year's sediment, are called a varve. Each varve, consisting of a light and a dark layer, represents one year's deposition of sediment. By digging down far enough, the earth scientist can expose and count the number of varves and thereby determine the age of the buried material.

A varve

The saltiness of ocean water is a clue to the approximate age of an ocean. First the scientists measure the salt in a given volume of ocean water. They then multiply that figure by the total estimated volume of water in the ocean to get the amount of all the salt in the entire ocean. Finally, by measuring the size and rate of flow of the rivers feeding into the ocean, they are able to estimate how much dissolved salt is added to the ocean each year.

Calculations done with these figures show that the world's oceans are about 500 million years old. The difficulty with this approach is that it is very approximate. It is unlikely, too, that the rate of increase of salt has stayed the same over millions of years.

Some fossil remains of plants or animals are of particular value in dating the past. These fossils are of plants or animals that lived for only a short period in the history of the earth. They are called index or guide fossils. If a rock is found with a guide fossil, the scientists can be quite sure when the rock was formed.

Earth scientists also use guide fossils in their search for oil and other minerals in the earth. They already know which particular fossils are usually found near deposits of oil. Similar fossils found during oil exploration are considered clues that oil might be in that area.

Measuring the age of rocks by their natural radioactivity gives much more exact figures than other methods. Because it is such an exact and reliable way of dating the past, it is popular among earth scientists.

Some rocks contain elements that are naturally radioactive. They are always decaying and emitting particles and rays. As the radioactive elements decay, they change and become different elements. In time, they become nonradioactive.

There is no way of knowing when a particular atom will emit a particle or ray. But it is known how long it will take for half the atoms within a sample of the element to decay and become nonradioactive. This figure is known as the half-life of the element. Each radioactive element has a

different half-life. Half-lives vary from a tiny fraction of a second up to many billions of years. Scientists believe that the half-life of an element is always the same. And they believe it has not changed at all throughout the earth's history.

Uranium, with a mass of 238, is a radioactive element that is often used to determine the geological age of rocks. It has a half-life of 4.5 billion years—that is, it takes 4 1/2 billion years for half of the radioactive uranium 238 to decay into nonradioactive lead, with a mass of 206.

Lead 206 is slightly different from ordinary lead. Scientists use the uranium–lead method to date igneous rocks that contain uranium 238 and lead 206. The comparative amounts of lead and uranium provide information on the age of the rock.

The actual formula is based on the fact that in one year 1/7,600,000,000th of the uranium in the original sample will have changed to lead.

Using this method, earth scientists have found rocks in South Africa that are nearly 3 1/2 billion years old. They have also found rocks in Canada over 2 1/2 billion years in age, and some in the Black Hills of South Dakota that are more than 1 1/2 billion years old.

Rubidium 87 is a radioactive element that decays into strontium and has a half-life of 49 billion years, longer even than that of uranium. The rubidium–strontium method is often used as a check on the uranium–lead method when both uranium and rubidium are found in the same rock.

Over the past few years, though, scientists have found

other radioactive elements that they can use for dating. One of the newest, and most important, radioactive methods uses the decay of radioactive potassium 40 into argon. Potassium is much more common than either of the other two elements. It is found in metamorphic rocks and not only in igneous rocks. This makes it possible to date many rocks that could not be dated by the uranium or rubidium methods.

Potassium 40 has a half-life of 1.3 billion years. Since it is so much shorter than the others, it can be used to date rocks that are as young as 1 1/2 million years old. In 1959, the potassium–argon method was used to date the ape-man found in Tanganyika, Africa, as being 1.75 million years old.

Earth scientists have still another radioactive method to date the remains of once-living plants or animals. All living beings take in carbon 14, a radioactive form of carbon that is found in the air. Their cells contain a tiny, fixed amount of this form of carbon. The half-life of carbon 14 is only 5,730 years.

As long as the plant or animal is alive, the amount of carbon 14 in its cells stays the same. Once the plant or animal dies, though, the amount of carbon 14 begins to drop because of radioactive decay. By measuring the remaining carbon 14, it is possible to tell when the living being died.

Carbon-14 dating works for animal or human remains, as well as for wood or other remains of plants. And it has been found accurate from about 1,000 years to 60,000 years in the past. Carbon-14 dating of samples of wood, for example, helped scientists decide that the last glacier of the most recent ice age disappeared from the United States about 11,000 years ago.

In 1977, researchers in Canada and the United States announced a new and better way to use carbon-14 dating. The old method determined the amount of carbon 14 in an object by counting the radioactive rays it emitted. The new method will detect the amount of carbon 14 directly, by using an atomic accelerator, such as a cyclotron.

The advantages of this new approach are that the measurement can be made with a smaller sample and in less time, and that it can be used to date objects as old as 100,000 years, instead of the 60,000-year maximum of the old method. Another possible benefit of this new approach is that it may be used to measure the amounts of other radioactive substances that will also help in dating objects from the past.

The story of the earth and of life on earth is one of continual change and development. Recent advances in earth science have brought us information about the earth's history that stretches back billions of years. This valuable knowledge helps us to understand even better our precious home in space. And it also helps us to prepare for the future by preserving the wealth and beauty of our planet earth.

FOR FURTHER READING

Berger, Melvin. *Energy from the Sun.* New York: Crowell, 1976.

——. *Jigsaw Continents.* New York: Coward, McCann, 1977.

Branley, Franklyn. *The Earth, Planet Number 3.* New York: Crowell, 1966.

Constant, Constantine. *The Student Earth Scientist Explores the Changing Earth.* New York: Richards Rosen, 1976.

Wyckoff, Jerome. *The Story of Geology.* Rev. ed. New York: Golden, 1976.

More advanced books:

Cloud, Treston. *Cosmos, Earth and Man.* New Haven: Yale University Press, 1978.

Heintze, Carl. *The Biosphere.* Nashville: Nelson, 1977.

Lanham, Url. *The Sapphire Planet.* New York: Columbia, 1978.

Ordway, Frederick. *Pictorial Guide to Planet Earth.* New York: Crowell, 1975.

Shurkin, Joel. *Update—Report on the Planet Earth.* Philadelphia: Westminster, 1976.

INDEX

MELVIN BERGER is the author of over sixty books for young readers, several of which have been named Outstanding Science Trade Books for Children by the National Science Teachers Association and the Children's Book Council.

A former teacher, Mr. Berger now devotes full time to his writing. He lives in Great Neck, New York, with his wife and two daughters.

GEORGE DEGRAZIO grew up in Colorado and received his M.F.A. from the University of Colorado in Boulder. Printmaker, illustrator, and one-time graphic arts teacher, he lives in the mountains in Idaho Springs with his wife, Lisa, and daughter, Sarah.